W9-CBR-342

SKYWALKERS

MOHAWK IRONWORKERS BUILD THE CITY

David Weitzman

Flash Point

Roaring Brook Press
New York

To All My Students of the
Round Valley Indian Tribes

Copyright © 2010 by David Weitzman
Published by Flash Point, an imprint of Roaring Brook Press
Roaring Brook Press is a division of Holtzbrinck Publishing Holdings Limited Partnership.
175 Fifth Avenue, New York, New York 10010
www.roaringbrookpress.com

Distributed in Canada by H. B. Fenn and Company Ltd.

Cataloging-in-Publication Data is on file at the Library of Congress
ISBN 978-1-59643-162-1

Roaring Brook Press books are available for special promotions and premiums.
For details contact: Director of Special Markets, Holtzbrinck Publishers.

First Edition September 2010
Book design by Edward Miller
Printed in August 2010 in the United States of America by RR Donnelley & Sons Company,
Harrisonburg, Virginia

10 9 8 7 6 5 4 3 2 1

Previous page: On the mooring mast of the Empire State Building, 1931. The mast was intended for the docking of dirigibles, but was never used.

This page: A team of workers haul on a rope to move a piece of heavy equipment above them.

CONTENTS

INTRODUCTION

Two hundred feet above the city, a new skyscraper slowly climbs toward the sky. A bare skeleton of steel I-beams is being assembled, floor by floor, by ironworkers.

On the street below, the weather is calm. But up here, high winds threaten to topple the workers. A sudden gust can knock them from their footing with its sheer force or send a fatal vibration through the beams on which they stand. And yet the men joke, laugh, stroll across the foot-wide beams as though they are on solid ground. To the people on the sidewalk, tiny as ants below, the skywalkers appear entirely unafraid. A hundred years ago, their grandfathers and great-grandfathers built the skyscrapers and bridges that surround them. Hundreds of years before that, their ancestors walked the rooflines of longhouses.

They are Mohawk Indians, and the story that led them from the longhouse villages to the urban landscape is part of a tradition stretching back thousands of years. But it is also the story of the American city. Of a moment when the cityscape, once built of wood, brick, and stone, found steel and reached for the sky.

For centuries, the tallest buildings were barely nine stories tall. But at the beginning of the twentieth century, engineers, such as John Roebling and James Eads, and architects, such as Louis Sullivan and Daniel Burnham, raced to design longer bridges and taller buildings. Americans were as familiar with these names as we are with the inventors of new Web and computer technology today. But, as is true in every age, mostly unsung workers toiled at the edge of the possible to construct the bridges and buildings those visionaries designed.

A connector sets a beam atop Rockefeller Center.

Among those who climbed high up into the iron and steel girders of bridges and skyscrapers to work in this new frontier were Mohawk Indians. Most of them came from communities in Canada—Kahnawake, Akwesasne, and Six Nations of the Grand River.

Performing dangerous work several hundred, if not several thousand, feet up in the air requires amazing concentration, courage, and grit—the very qualities the Mohawks would ascribe to their ancestors throughout their long history. That tradition continues today with the hundreds of Mohawk ironworkers on one-hundred-plus-story skyscrapers and mile-long bridges going up all over the world.

above: Mohawk ironworkers on the United Nations Building, completed in 1950. From left to right: Angus Mitchell, Joe Jocks, and unidentified worker.

left: Ironworkers Jay Jacobs (foreground) and Sparky Rice working on a steel beam. The national flag is always placed at the highest point on the building.

PEOPLE OF THE FLINT

"We had a reputation as rivermen and ironworking was a different kind of work. We didn't have the tools or traditional skills to fall back on—it was our introduction to the industrial age."
—Conway Jocks, Kannawake ironworker

To be accurate, they are not really "Mohawks." The Indians of southern New England called the tribe the Mohowawogs, which means "man-eaters"—and by all accounts they did eat some of their captives taken in war. Early Dutch and English explorers heard the word as "Mohawks." The tribe calls themselves the *Kanien'kéhaka*—People of the Flint. (The "k" is pronounced like our "g".) But for 400 years now, since the arrival of the Europeans, "Mohawks" is what they have been called, and though they may not refer to themselves that way, they do not mind if others do.

The origins of the people are lost in time, but the plentiful archaeological record around upstate New York goes back at least 4,000 years. By some estimates, ancestors of modern-day Mohawks lived on the same land as long as 12,000 years ago.

From the beginning, the Mohawks were a people who fostered cooperation and community effort. They were leaders in establishing the League of the Iroquois, a confederation of Indian nations in the New York region founded sometime in the 1500s to maintain peace among themselves and with surrounding nations. The names of the original Five Nations describe the lands each inhabited as well as their responsibilities as peacekeepers: Onöndowága (Seneca), People of the Great Hill, and Keepers of the Western Door; Guyohkohnyo (Cayuga),

People of the Mucky Land; Onöñda'gega (Onondaga), People of the Mountains; Onyota'a:ka (Oneida), People of the Granite; and Kanien'kéhaka (Mohawk), People of the Flint, and Keepers of the Eastern Door. Later, the Tuscarora, Shirt Wearing People, were invited to join the confederation, making it Six Nations. The coming together of six nations to form a confederation in the spirit of peace and mutual protection at this early date was, in the view of Dr. Robert Muller, an Assistant Secretary General of the United Nations, "perhaps the oldest effort for disarmament in world history."

So successful were the laws and treaties that held together the Grand Council of the United Haudenosaunee (or Iroquois) that that many of its ideas were adopted by America's founding fathers. But not all of them; in some ways the laws of the Iroquois Confederacy were surprisingly progressive when compared to the laws of the United States. While Iroquois women from earliest times participated at all levels of the government, from the village councils up to the Grand Council, the Constitution did not even give American women the right to vote. It was well over a century before women were granted this right. And even then, many decades passed before American women were elected to office.

Americans were impressed not only with Mohawk institutions but also their respectful attitude toward each other. Joseph Bloomfield, a soldier of the Revolution and, later, Governor of New Jersey, left this account of the Mohawks meeting in council.

> The Character of the Indians is striking. They are grave even to sadness, upon any serious Occasion; observant of those in Company, respectful to the old, of a temper cool and deliberate, by which they are never in haste to speak before they have thought well on the matter & are sure the person who spoke before them has finished all he had to say.
>
> Nothing is more edifying than their behavior in their public Councils & Assemblies; every man there is heard in his turn, According to his Years, Wisdom, or service to his Country, have ranked him. Not a Word, not a Whisper, not a murmur is heard from the rest, whilst He speaks; no indecent condemnation, no ill-timed applause.

Like most ancient cultures, the Mohawks had no formal system of writing. Their history and traditions were passed down from generation to generation through the spoken word. During the winter months, as storms raged outside, the village storyteller would gather the children around the warmth of the longhouse fire and, accompanied by the crackling, sputtering flames and the flickering shadows, entertain them with exciting tales of their ancestors. The children sat entranced as the storyteller's voice went from a whisper to shouts and cries. With flailing arms and great leaps, he would reenact battles of men and gods and then, just as suddenly, drop to an almost inaudible hush again. As the children grew up, sitting winter after winter around the storyteller's fire, they learned about the Great Spirit and the origins of the people, animals, plants, and the world itself. They learned their customs, proper behavior, and their eventual roles as men and women. And they were expected to learn all this by heart so that they could tell the stories to *their* children. Each storyteller made the tales his own and, as times changed, so did the stories.

Life changed drastically with the arrival of the Europeans. Many Mohawks were converted to Christianity, and the priests forbade them to tell their creation stories, even to speak their own language. Today, the storytellers are gone, and many of their tales forgotten. All that is left of that history are bits and fragments collected many years ago from the distant memories of the elderly.

Most of what we do know about traditional Mohawk life comes down to us in the journals of Dutch explorers who traveled through their lands in the 1600s and 1700s. Among them were keen observers who were curious about the native peoples they encountered. They were able to overcome their European prejudices and leave detailed, accurate, and candid accounts of what they saw and experienced. These accounts are particularly valuable because they are a record of life in the Mohawk villages before the intrusion of the Europeans. At that time, *Kanienke*, the Land of the Flint, extended from the St. Lawrence River in the north to the Mohawk River in the south, and from the Hudson River Valley and Lake Champlain west all the way to the Great Lakes—in all, more than 6 million acres.

THE LONGHOUSE PEOPLE

The Iroquois were collectively known as the Haudenosaunee (sometimes written Hootenosonni), "they build longhouses," and first impressions of encounters with the Mohawks always included descriptions of the villages and massive buildings where they lived. Europeans were so impressed by the longhouses that they referred to them as "castles." Adding to their impressive size was their defensive placement high up on palisades. A Dutch explorer, Adriaen Cornelissen van der Donck, described his visit to a Mohawk settlement in 1634:

> We came into their first castle that stood on a high hill. There were 36 houses, row on row in the manner of streets, so that we could easily pass through. These houses are constructed and covered with the bark of trees, and are mostly flat above. Some are 100, 90, or 80 steps long; 22 or 23 feet high. There were many wooden gables on the houses that were painted with all sorts of animals. In each house there were four, five, or six places for fires and cooking. There were also some interior doors made of split planks furnished with iron hinges. In some

Eleuation des Cabannes Sauvages

An engraving by a French explorer depicts a longhouse, ca. 1600.

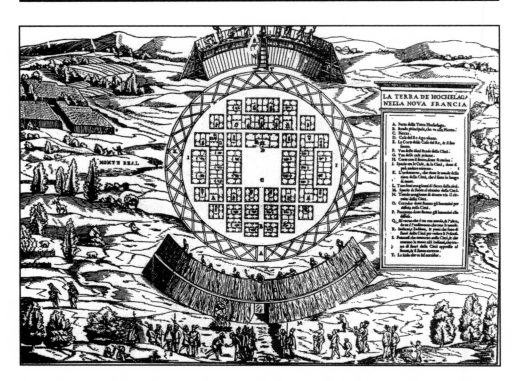

An idealized French map of an Iroquois community shows longhouses arranged in a central cluster, surrounded by sections of palisades protecting the village. In reality, the longhouses were aligned in two rows surrounded by the palisades.

houses we also saw ironwork: iron chains, bolts, harrow teeth, iron hoops, spikes. Most of the people were out hunting for bear and deer. These houses were full of grain that they call *onesti* and we corn; indeed, some held 300 or 400 skipples [bushels]. We ate here many baked and boiled pumpkins that they call *anonsira*.

The size and shape of each longhouse reflected the size and shape of the Mohawk family that lived there. Theirs was a matrilineal society in which families were linked through the women. When a child was born, he or she became part of the mother's clan and the center of attention of a large, extended family. At the head of each clan—Bear, Wolf, or Turtle—was the clan mother, usually the oldest woman, and her council, made up of women of all ages. It's still that way today. The clan mother makes all the important decisions. One of her biggest responsibilities is to choose the male leader, called "Caretaker of the Peace," who, in turn, represents the clan in the government of the Six Nations. The clan mother also gives names to the newborn children, a tradition described in this story by anthropologist Alexander Goldenweiser:

> She was born in a bark house. Her mother, Rising-sun, was surprised as she looked at the little face. The child was the image of her great-grandmother, Rising-sun's mother's mother, whom she had often seen when she herself was a little girl. Hanging-flower had been a great medicine woman in her day, and the fame of her art had spread far and wide.
>
> Soon after this, when Rising-sun had regained her health and vigor, she called on Clear-as-a-brook, Keeper of the Names of the Bear Clan, to which Rising-sun belonged. From her the mother learned that another Hanging-flower, a remote relative of Rising-sun, of whom she remembered having heard, had recently died and that her name had been "put away in a box." The mother knew now that nothing stood in the way of the realization of her desire: Hanging-flower was to be the name of the little girl.

All the members of the clan—parents, sisters and brothers, aunts and uncles, cousins and grandparents—lived together in a longhouse. But the Mohawks didn't use these kinship terms. To a child growing up among an extended family, every woman in the longhouse was "mother," every man was "father," and all the children were "brothers" and "sisters." Adults then were mother and father to all the children of the clan. The longhouse got longer as the extended family got larger.

Inside the longhouse, arranged along both sides, were sections set aside for each nuclear family (made up of a mother, father, and their biological children). Down the middle were the "places for fire" shared by families opposite each other. On the walls were raised sleeping platforms with storage space underneath.

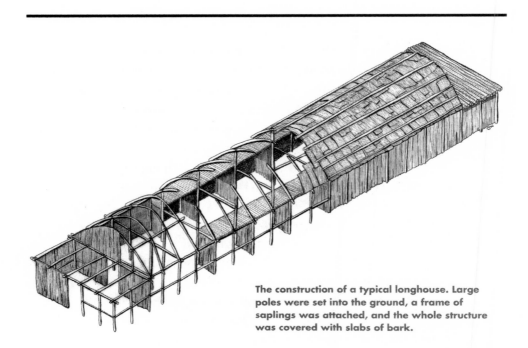

The construction of a typical longhouse. Large poles were set into the ground, a frame of saplings was attached, and the whole structure was covered with slabs of bark.

Wherever they visited a longhouse, the early explorers were welcomed. The families would gather around them, curious about the strange blond people in their midst. Gifts were exchanged, the Indians giving valuable beaver pelts and the explorers iron tools. And there was always a feast in their honor. Not only were the visitors well fed—venison, bear, turkey, baked and boiled pumpkins, salmon, trout, perch, and pike—they were always sent on their way with ample dried meats for their long journeys afoot between villages. Along the way, they observed Mohawk farms:

> Their cultivated lands are . . . between the hills, on the margin or along the side of rivers, brooks, or creeks, very flat and level, without a single bush or tree upon them, of a black sandy soil which is four and sometimes five or six feet deep, which can hardly be exhausted. They cultivate it year after year, without manure, for many years. It yields large crops of wheat.

The women and young girls of the longhouses worked together cultivating the fields, planting, and harvesting the Three Sisters—corn, beans, and squash. The Three Sisters were grown together on a mound of earth about a foot high. Corn was planted first on top of the mound. When each stalk was about a foot high, beans were planted next to it, so the vines could wind upward around the tall corn. Squash was also planted on the mound, at the foot of the corn. Fruits and nuts were also gathered from the forest. Though it was the men's responsibility to hunt and fish, they often helped the women with the planting and harvest.

Several travelers had an opportunity to watch the Mohawks at play, commenting on their physical strength and skill. One marveled at the Mohawk canoe:

> . . . made of the bark of trees, and the Indians have many of them for the purpose of making their journeys.
>
> It was fifteen or sixteen feet or more in length. It was so light that two men could easily carry it, as the Indians do in going from one stream or lake to another. They come in such canoes from Canada, and from places so distant we know not where. Four or five of them stepped into this one and rowed lustily through the water with great speed, and when they came back with the current they seemed to fly.

Another described their games—and penchant for betting—played especially during the harvest when everyone stayed close to the village.

> And during this time the men play almost everyday a game which consists of making a ball fly. Each player is supplied with a sort of racquet about four feet and six inches long, somewhat curved at the end, and netted with a bowstring, which is used to throw the ball. The player who succeeds in catching the ball with this instrument, juggling it while preventing others from touching it, until he can perform a given number of turns in a large field is victorious. These turns require dexterity and agility in running;

we have attended one game that lasted two and a half hours, in which a large sum was at stake on both sides.

The game they describe is lacrosse. It was played on a field between goals, 600 to 1,200 feet apart, depending on the skill and number of players. The goals were marked by pairs of upright poles about 12 feet high, anywhere from 9 to 27 feet apart, with a cord strung between them. Two goalkeepers, or "door guards," were positioned in front of each goal. The game began with the teams deciding how many points would determine a win. The two team captains stood in the middle of the field holding the ball between their two sticks. After that, anything and everything was allowed, and it was a dangerous, rough-and-tumble game. The egg-shaped wooden ball had to be thrown or carried through the goal posts, defended by tough guys wielding big sticks. Tripping, holding, and charging were fair play. Players were often severely injured, and a few even killed.

Although the longhouse culture disappeared centuries ago, many of its values and ways of life (and lacrosse), Mohawks will tell you, are still very much alive. Visit a Mohawk reserve today and your first impression will be of a people deeply committed to family, friends, and community, with a close connection to the land, who choose collaboration over competition. All the children are the concern of all the adults. As one modern Kahnawake, Conway Jocks, puts it: "We always did things as a group, from hunting and farming to warfare and trade to *ironworking*. The idea is that whenever any one of us finds good work, others are encouraged to share that opportunity for the common good."

In the beginning, the Mohawks had learned cooperation out of necessity. Surrounded by warring peoples, they joined scattered camps together into villages better able to defend themselves. Even as they formed larger villages, the cooperative spirit held. Tightly knit communities also became their best defense against unfriendly Europeans.

The Mohawks, being the easternmost of the Six Nations, came into early and frequent contact with Europeans. The Mohawk Valley had been for thousands of years one of the principal pathways between the Atlantic Coast and inland America. First encounters were with explorers, then French and Basque fishermen and traders, and then the Dutch and English.

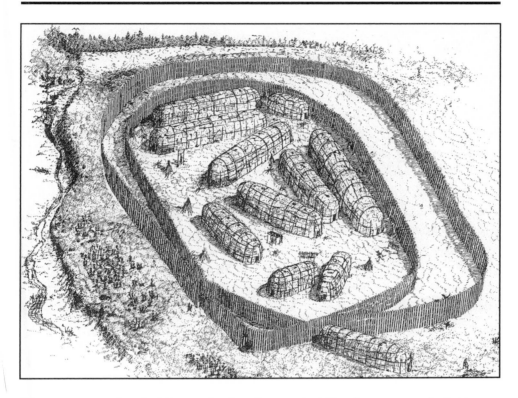

A contemporary archaeologist's reconstruction of a pre-colonial longhouse community. Even though the structures disappeared long ago, reconstructions are possible because careful excavation reveals the filled-in postholes.

In the end, it wasn't the intruders' guns that killed off the Mohawks; it was their diseases. Epidemics of measles and smallpox, brought by the French and the Dutch, swept through the Iroquois nation in 1633. Nothing in their long history had been as devastating. The Mohawk population simply collapsed, dropping from almost 8,000 to about 2,000 in just a few months. They left their isolated, disease-infested villages and the hundreds of new graves and came together in three large new communities along the borders of current-day Canada and New York.

The Europeans who traded with the Mohawk communities quickly developed an impression that Mohawk men were attracted to danger. "They will walk over deep brooks and creeks on the smallest poles, and that without fear and concern," surveyor John Lawson observed in 1714; "an Indian will walk on the ridge of a barn or house and look down the gable end and spit on the ground, as unconcerned as if he were walking on terra firma."

Eventually, many of the men hired out as *voyageurs*, a word used by the French Canadian fur traders to describe the boatmen who navigated boatloads of furs through hundreds of miles of white-water rapids. It was dangerous work, but profitable; each pelt brought a gold dollar. Stylish European gentlemen of the day required fur trimming on their coats, and hats of felted beaver skins. The rich profits attracted young Frenchmen who canoed deep into the wilderness and spent the winter hunting and trapping with the Indians. In the spring, as soon as the ice on the lakes, rivers, and streams broke up, they loaded the boats, each with up to 600 beaver skins, and rowed out into the raging waters. The Mohawk boatmen thrilled to every danger and challenge, guiding the boats from the Great Lakes, down rushing creeks and tributaries of the Ottawa, over the tricky, deadly Lachine Rapids, and along the St. Lawrence to a chain of small trading posts—Port Royal, Montreal, and Quebec—which grew into towns and cities. These little settlements were another place Europeans came together with the Indians who canoed their valuable furs to the trading posts and bartered for axes, iron kettles, blankets, muskets, knives, scissors, sewing needles, and cloth.

Several generations of Mohawks stayed on the water. Some took on the scary job of riding rafts of logs harvested in the woods down to the mills. "We had a reputation as river men," Conway Jocks tells us, "some of whom were pilots on the steamers going from Kahnawake to Lachine and Montreal." But by the late 1800s all of that would begin to change, and, once again, Mohawk men would adapt to their new circumstances.

A BRIDGE TO THE FUTURE

"Climbing that first high tower,
and standing on that first high beam,
is a rite of passage into a fellowship,
son follows father up into the air."
—*Eugene Skye, Mohawk ironworker*

The change came in 1886. That was the year the Dominion Bridge Company began construction of the Victoria Bridge across the St. Lawrence.

When it was complete, it would connect the island of Montreal, Canada's largest seaport, with the country's vast inland region and the United States to the south. The railroad would move timber from the Ottawa River Valley, wheat, barley, oats, and flax from the rich, black soil of the long-grass prairies, and coal from Athabasca and the Rocky Mountains to the west.

But the bridge had a larger purpose, too. There had always been several Canadas—upper and lower, English and French, Protestant and Catholic, Canada west and Canada east—beset by rebellions and contention, especially between English- and French-speaking Canadians (some of which continues to this day). By the mid-1800s, though still widely divided, the separate factions were talking about confederation under a constitution similar to that of the United States. Railroads were seen as a way of making this confederation work, of joining Canadians together. Kahnawake suddenly took on new importance.

Since 1852, a railroad had connected Moore's Junction, New York, to a wharf in Kahnawake. Here, passengers booked passage on the ferries that steamed back and forth across the St. Lawrence, between Kahnawake and Montreal. Goods were taken off freight cars and loaded onto steam freighters. But this arrangement had become inadequate. There were just too many passengers and too much freight to move by ferry. In addition, the unloading and loading of freight from wagons and freight cars onto the steamers and off again was costly and time consuming. And so, business interests in Montreal began plans for a railroad bridge. In 1850, the Grand Trunk Railway hired an English engineer, James Hodges, who would be responsible for designing the bridge, buying all the necessary materials, arranging for their delivery to the site, hiring laborers, and overseeing the construction.

The Mohawks found themselves in the right place at the right time. The timbers for the bridge—it was a composite bridge of wood and iron—could be delivered by Mohawk river pilots. The stone for the abutments could be gotten at a quarry close to the bridge site, owned by the people of Kahnawake. The stone would be cut and dressed by men of the village. However, Hodges would need the approval of the chiefs to buy their stone. He describes that meeting in his construction records.

> After having inspected several quarries, a visit was paid to Caughnawaga [Kahnawake] where very fine stone was found. The lands from which it was obtainable were, however, in the possession of the Indians, and it became necessary to treat with the chiefs of the tribe who held its possession.
>
> At the appointed time, accompanied by an interpreter, I was ushered into the presence of the assembled chiefs. To a number of twelve or thirteen they were waiting my arrival in a wooden shanty. After so much pomp and ceremony as had been expanded on preliminaries, I certainly expected to have met chiefs ornamented after the manner of those in [James Fenimore] Cooper's novels, with paint, and feathers, and prepared before they proceeded in council, to offer me the calumet [pipe] of peace.
>
> At first the chiefs exhibited a great reluctance to treat. I endeavored to discover the obstacle and found they considered my youth a serious disadvantage. Upon reassuring them, however, through the interpreter, that I was not less than forty, and by pointing out the grey hairs with which time had adorned

me, I managed to persuade them that I was worthy of the honor of their respect. Preliminaries thus over, the other arrangements were easy, more so as the terms proposed were liberal. The treaty was adjusted and after shaking hands all around, the meeting was dissolved and all parties were satisfied.

Half an hour after this interview I found myself with one of the chiefs in a canoe, paddling off to a mail packet [boat] in which I was to return to Montreal. The chief, although at the interview exceedingly taciturn and apparently quite ignorant of English, was now sufficiently garrulous and evidently a fluent speaker of the language. He was a pilot for the Rapids of Lachine, which the steamer was about to shoot.

To the men of Kahnawake, the new bridge posed a not-yet-realized dilemma. Yes, they would sell stone to the Grand Trunk Railway, and Kanien'kéhaka would be paid to cut and transport stone from theirs and other quarries. They would be paid to transport timbers down river to the bridge site as they had been doing for generations. And, since one of the bridge's abutments would be on reserve land, there was a promise of work. But what would happen when the bridge was completed? The trains would begin running from New York and lands to the west right into Montreal's town center, and the river steamers and their pilots would become unnecessary. What's more, along with every other kind of good, the railroad would bring furs from the interior of Canada, which meant that the daring Kanien'kéhaka voyageurs and river pilots would soon be out of work.

But the construction proceeded as planned. The timber rafts arrived on schedule at the wharfs after their long journey from distant forests, and the quarrymen and river pilots delivered the cut stone to the construction site.

Kahnawake elder Tom Diabo told historian David Blanchard a story he learned from his grandfather about what happened next.

Back in those days we Indians used to work on the river, delivering big ships over the rapids to Montreal and Kingston. Well, when they was building the Victoria Bridge, not the one there now, the old one, men from town got work delivering stone from the quarry over behind Blind Lady Hill to the masons on the bridge site.

You know how Mohawks love to build things. So when the men from town were watching the bridge get built, some of the younger guys just climbed right up to take a closer look at how it was done. The Frenchmen they had working there was so scared that they had to hold on to everything they could so they wouldn't fall off. That engineer wasn't getting anything done with so many scared Frenchmen working for him. Of course, the guys from town wasn't scared. They just walked along the supports looking the job over, and checking out how the job was done.

The engineer saw this and wanted to hire the Indians, but there was a problem, cuz most of the men only talked Indian. So he hired a whole crew of guys from town, with a foreman who could talk English and French and Indian.

This is how we got into the construction business.

Construction wasn't all the Kanien'kéhaka learned from the bridge. It also introduced them to show business. In August 1860, the Prince of Wales, the future King Edward of England, came to Montreal for the bridge opening ceremonies. Sir George Simpson, governor of the Hudson's Bay Company, invited the men of Kahnawake to a reception honoring the prince at his home on the river. As the party stood looking out over the river toward Kahnawake, suddenly there appeared ten huge birch bark canoes flying across the water paddled by seventy-six Kanien'kéhaka in war paint and feathers, dazzling the prince and guests with their boating skills. At this, the prince and his party boarded the royal barge to be rowed out to the canoes. Here's how one observer described it.

When the barge carrying the prince and his suite pushed off from Lachine, the flotilla of canoes darted out abreast to meet it, keeping time to the cadence of a boatman's song. The line opened in the middle, as if to let the royal barge pass, but suddenly wheeling around formed abreast again, with the prince in the centre, and thus proceeded to the landing place at Dorval.

Towards evening, Sir George Simpson, an expert with canoe and paddle, directed the Indian voyageurs in the execution of another series of movements on the water. Then the flotilla carrying the Prince of Wales . . . and the rest of the distinguished visitors, crossed over Lake St. Louis to Caughnawaga [Kahnawake] and, after passing along the entire length of the village bank where the Indian population were lined up to cheer the royal procession, returned to Lachine.

"And that display," Conrad Jocks relates, "sparked another communal tradition—Indian entertainers." News of the bridge opening festivities spread quickly throughout Europe. Mohawks were invited to put on an exhibition of traditional crafts, lacrosse, and paddling at the Paris Universal Exposition of 1867 and, the following year, similar exhibitions in London and other cities. Mohawk entertainers were sought after to perform in Wild West shows that toured the United States and Europe. But, instead of enacting scenes of Mohawk life, they played the parts of Plains Indians, which were of greater interest to American and European audiences. Conrad Jocks's mother performed on stages all over the country up until the 1930s when the popularity of Wild West shows began to decline.

AGILE AS GOATS

The workers on the Victoria Bridge had, unknowingly, begun a new chapter in the life of the Kanien'kéhaka. If their reputation for doing the dangerous work of bridge building was not established quite yet, it soon would be. Another railroad bridge, built by the Canadian Pacific Railway in 1889, would elevate them from laborers to skilled ironworkers. (Ironworkers are the men and women who build steel structures, as opposed to steelworkers, who make the steel.)

The southern *abutment* for this bridge would also sit on reserve land and, in exchange, the Dominion Bridge Company agreed that Kanien'kéhaka would be hired as day laborers to unload materials. The men did not stay put for long, as an official of the D.B.C. recalled.

> They were dissatisfied with this arrangement and would come out on the bridge itself every chance they got. It was quite impossible to keep them off. As the work progressed, it became apparent to all concerned that these Indians were very odd in that they did not have any fear of heights. If not watched, they would climb up into the spans and walk around up there as cool and collected as the toughest of our riveters, most of whom at that period were old sailing-ship men especially picked for their experience working aloft.
>
> These Indians were agile as goats. They would walk on a narrow beam high up in the air with nothing below but the river, which is rough there and ugly to look down on, and it wouldn't mean any more to them than walking on the solid ground. They seemed immune to the noise of the riveting, which goes right through you and is often enough in itself to make newcomers to construction feel sick and dizzy.
>
> They were inquisitive about the riveting and were continually bothering their foremen by requesting that they be allowed to take a crack at it. This happens to be the most dangerous work in all of construction and the highest paid. Men who want to do it are rare and men who can do it are even rarer, and in good construction years there are sometimes not enough of them to go around.
>
> We decided it would be mutually advantageous to see what these Indians could do, so we picked out some and gave them a little training, and it turned out that putting riveting tools in their hands was like putting ham with eggs. In other words, they were naturally born bridgemen.

There are no records showing how many Kanien'kéhaka were trained, but apparently at least enough to make three riveting gangs of four men. Soon, the men of Kahnawake began heading for the bridges and walking the iron. The young men came to work to apprentice with the older more experienced bridgemen.

The Victoria Bridge carried the first trains of the Grand Trunk Railway across the St. Lawrence River.

CONNECTIONS: WOOD, IRON, AND STEEL

"I have a name for this town [New York]. I don't know if anybody said it before, but I call this town the City of Man-made Mountains. And we're all part of it, and it gives you a good feeling—you're a kind of mountain builder."
–Danny Montour, Kahnawake ironworker

It is unlikely that the Mohawks or, for that matter, any of the bridgemen of the late 1800s realized the vital role they were playing in a technological revolution.

It's like that in every age. When television, personal computers, and then cell phones first appeared, few people understood their importance or foresaw their impact on our lives. Today, they are so common that we no longer think of them as "electronic marvels"—we can't even remember what life was like without them.

The engineering marvels to which the Mohawks first contributed their skills over a century ago are today so commonplace that we hardly notice them. Frameworks of I-beams climbing a hundred stories toward the sky and bridges soaring across great expanses of water are such a part of our landscape that few of us take even a moment to look up and wonder. But a hundred years ago, a building of ten or twenty stories would have been front-page news all over the country, if not the world, and drawn gawking, awestruck crowds.

That technological revolution was actually two revolutions happening at the same time. If you look closely at history, you discover that many seemingly separate events are actually entwined. One development leads to the next, and that one causes another, and another comes as a response to that one, on and on.

The bridges and tall buildings the Mohawks helped build were the result of just such a chain of events. The challenge to engineers in the 1800s to build sturdier, longer bridges and taller, more fireproof buildings led to the search for new building materials. These new materials then made possible the construction of even taller buildings and longer spans, which then spurred the search for even stronger materials, which made possible much longer bridges and taller skyscrapers, which . . . well, you get the idea. The cause of all this change was the development of railroad locomotives.

For thousands of years, the heaviest load a bridge builder could imagine had been a wooden wagon, pulled by oxen—a few tons. Wooden bridges worked fine over small streams and rivers. In most places, the road just went down to the water's edge at the shallowest fording spot and continued up the bank on the other side. Wide rivers might be spanned with bridges of stone, but this required immense amounts of expensive labor—and danger. The longer the false work (the wooden framework temporarily supporting the stone work until it was completed) stood in the riverbed, the greater the chance it and the workers on it would be swept away by a flood.

Then, beginning in the 1830s, that all changed. Throughout the nineteenth century, British inventors built steam locomotives, slow and ponderous at first, but increasing in speed with each new experimental design. For all of human history, the highest speed anyone had ever attained was astride a horse—ten to twelve miles an hour. Then, on September 15, 1830, the *Rocket*, a little steam engine built by George Stephenson and his nineteen-year-old son, Robert, sped across the English countryside at nearly thirty miles an hour! Very soon the Stephensons were building locomotives that could travel a mile a minute.

TIMBER-TRUSS BRIDGES

George Stephenson and Company built their first steam locomotive for a railroad in America in 1831. At about 11,000 pounds, the *John Bull* could still run safely over sturdy timber bridges. But by the 1860s, locomotives were ten times heavier—over 100,000 pounds. Bridge builders had to contend with the stresses of shifting cargo loads and speeding locomotives swaying side to side, accelerating and decelerating more violently the faster they went.

The challenges for builders became more complex as the number of variables increased. Eventually, they had to consider the weight of more than one locomotive on the bridge. The practice of double-heading long, heavy freight trains meant that a single span might have to support two locomotives coupled together. If the bridge carried two tracks, then there was the possibility that as many as four or more locomotives speeding in both directions might be on the bridge at the same time. As spans got longer, not only were there these many locomotives but scores of freight and passenger cars as well. Builders

A timber-truss bridge under construction in 1890, one of the earliest projects employing Mohawk workmen. The trusses were supported by temporary false-work timbers until they could stand on their own.

now had to consider the stresses of loads approaching a million pounds. It had become impractical, if not impossible, to build wooden bridges that could withstand not only such great weight, but all the movement and vibration. And there was another problem: steam locomotives threw off sparks and cinders, often setting the countryside and wooden bridges afire. Wooden bridges had truly reached the limit of their usefulness.

BRIDGES OF IRON

Bridge builders needed to find a material that would give them strength, rigidity, and resistance to fire. And they didn't have to look far. The quest for taller, fireproof structures had led to the use of iron instead of wood for the frames of large buildings. The story of how iron buildings led to the skyscraper is for another chapter, but suffice it to say iron had proven to be an excellent building material and was becoming less expensive as it became more available. By the 1900s, America was on the way to being the world's leading iron producer.

To make iron, ore is dug from the ground and smelted, or heated in a furnace until the iron becomes molten and flows out of the rock. Iron contains, among other minerals, carbon, and it is the amount of carbon in the iron that determines its strength.

Cast iron contains about three pounds of carbon in every hundred pounds of iron. Cast iron is brittle, easily broken when bent or twisted, and it rusts quickly. But it works well under compression, supporting heavy loads. A good use for cast iron is the heavy columns supporting buildings.

Wrought iron is cast iron worked under a huge hammer, reducing the amount of carbon. The hammering changes the structure of the iron, making it softer and therefore not as brittle as cast iron. It also makes it more resistant to rust. Wrought iron makes better beams and rods that are used under tension. Unlike cast iron, wrought iron can resist bending and twisting pressures.

Imagine a powerful machine that could grip both ends of a one-inch thick stick of wood and then pull in opposite directions until the stick came apart. Now imagine putting into that machine a one-inch thick iron bar, which is pulled

An early ironwork cantilever span showing the anchor arm (far left) and cantilever arm.

until it too snaps in two. Such a machine is used to determine a material's tensile strength, the force it takes to pull it apart, to make it fail. Four locomotives on a bridge exert the same kind of forces. Knowing the tensile strength helps builders determine which material and how much of it is needed to create a safe structure.

Iron's tensile strength is much greater than that of wood. Building lumber, for example, has a tensile strength of about 2,500 pounds per square inch. The tensile strength of iron is over 18,000 pounds per square inch. Iron was clearly the answer—but a temporary one.

BRIDGES OF STEEL

Toward the end of the nineteenth century, locomotives were approaching 200,000 pounds. A bridge built around 1900 would, in just twenty years, be carrying the combined weight of several locomotives, each weighing 500,000 pounds. By the 1940s, there would be locomotives weighing almost a million pounds. And they were attaining incredible speeds, over a hundred miles an hour. On May 10, 1893, *Empire State Express* locomotive No. 999 was clocked at 112.5 miles per hour, breaking all records of all time. Then, in 1905, a Pennsylvania Railroad locomotive reached 127.1 miles per hour.

From the 1860s to the 1880s Americans had built more miles of railroads than the whole rest of the world combined. At the end of the Civil War, there were about 40,000 miles of railroad tracks; just twenty-five years later, in 1890, there were 163,000 miles. Tens of thousands of bridges were needed to expand the rail system. As Americans and the railroads moved out west, they encountered wide rivers like the Hudson, the Ohio, the Mississippi, the Arkansas, and the Missouri, some of the most difficult barriers ever encountered.

These were not only wide, wild rivers but also navigable rivers, heavily traveled by steamboats carrying goods and passengers. Steamboat captains, guided by their charts, were careful to stay in the rivers' deep channels to avoid running aground in shallow waters. Fast-flowing rapids and unpredictable currents made it tricky, if not impossible, for the huge boats to maneuver between obstacles like bridge footings, or piers, out in the middle of the river. If the railroads were going to build bridges over the rivers, the steamboat companies demanded a clear channel—the distance between bridge footings—a thousand feet wide.

But the longest clear span in America at the time, the bridge over the Hudson River at Poughkeepsie, New York, was only 548 feet. Engineers stretched their imaginations and skills to design clear spans longer than they had ever before. To do so, they would have to use new materials to build new truss designs.

Steel, with only about one pound of carbon to every hundred pounds of iron, has all the qualities of both cast and wrought iron but is immensely stronger and more resistant to wear. *Alloyed* with small amounts of other elements, steel becomes even tougher. Today we speak of space age metals like titanium and vanadium, but a century ago the metals of the future were alloys of steel.

Steel had been around for centuries, used in the best knives and swords, but it could only be made in small quantities. Then, in 1856, an English inventor, Henry Bessemer, came up with a process of making what came to be known as Bessemer steel. Simply put, oxygen was blown through the molten iron, burning out most of the carbon and impurities. Huge Bessemer converters soon made steel both plentiful and inexpensive. The bridges for the new century would be constructed of alloys of steel with tensile strengths of up to 80,000 pounds per square inch.

Mills began producing steel beams on a massive scale. The beams were then transported to job sites, where workers such as the Mohawks began the hard work of realizing the engineer's vision. It was their job to maneuver the heavy steel beams into place. And, even more difficult, to join them together to form the larger structure.

The key to building with steel proved to be rivets. Riveting is a complicated process but, simply put, here's how it works: Holes are made in the two pieces of metal, and the pieces are held together, usually with bolts, so that the holes are lined up. A rivet is heated in a charcoal fire until it becomes red-hot and soft, and then pushed through the holes, so that the head of the rivet is on one side and the long shank is sticking out the other. The shank of the rivet is then hammered down against the metal and shaped into a neat button, just like the other end. As the rivet cools, it contracts, clamping the two pieces of metal

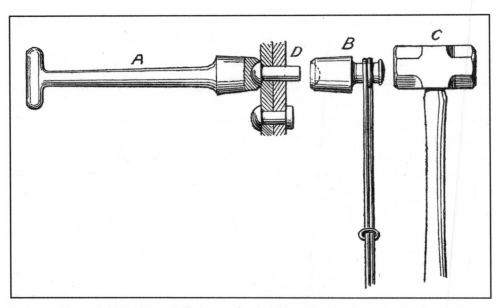

Tools used for manual riveting. While one worker held the dolly bar (A) against the head of the hot rivet (D), another held the cup (B) against the shank, and a third hammered against the cup, forming a rounded head.

tightly together. It seems simple, but done by hand it required a lot of skill.

In the early days, there were no scientific instruments, no electron microscopes, to let engineers actually see and understand the structure and chemistry of the metals they were working with. Much depended on the instincts and common sense of the engineer and the skill of the worker. The correct heat for the rivet was determined by its color—a deep cherry red. The cooled rivet was tested by striking it with a hammer. If the struck rivet made just the right ringing sound and held firm, it was good. But if striking the rivet produced a dull thud or the head loosened, the rivet was removed and another one put in.

The work required highly skilled workers who had to serve a long apprenticeship. A young boy, perhaps twelve years old, would begin as the forge boy who tended the forge and, over several years, work his way up to the most skilled position, riveter. His progress was not just a matter of experience. He would have to grow into a powerful adult to swing the heavy hammer and pound rivets through the long workday.

Imagine this work high up on a bridge or skyscraper. Rivets were heated in the hot coals of a small forge connected to a hand-operated bellows to keep the coals glowing and hot. A forge boy oversaw the heating, ensuring that the rivets were not overheated or "burnt," which weakened the metal and the finished joint.

The pieces being riveted were first assembled by a crew of platers, who installed a few "fitting-up" bolts to temporarily hold the pieces in position and draw them together as tightly as possible. The forge boy picked up one rivet at a time and threw it on the ground to knock off any clinkers (coals or ash). He passed it on to a carrier who dipped the tip in water, cooling the end in

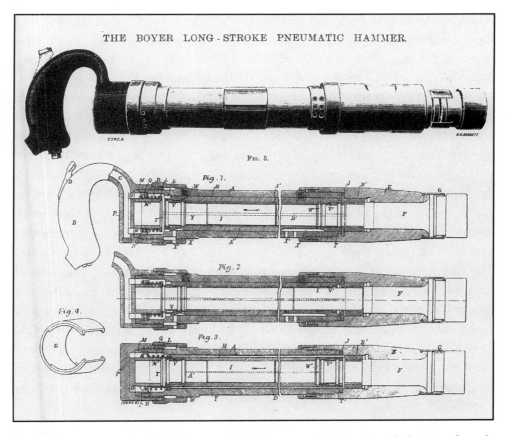

THE BOYER LONG-STROKE PNEUMATIC HAMMER.

Fig. 5.

Fig. 1.

Fig. 2.

Fig. 4.

Fig. 3.

The first Boyer pneumatic riveting hammer, 1898. The compressed air enters the hammer through a rubber hose attached to the handle. When the riveter squeezes the lever (D) with his thumb, the air drives the piston (I) and the riveting tools back and forth rapidly against the rivet shank.

comparison to the shank. The carrier then ran to the holder-on, who pushed it through the hole in the two overlapping members. While he held a dolly bar—a heavy sledgehammer with an indentation in the head to fit over the rivet—against the head, a pair of riveters struck alternating blows on the shank. Since the end of the rivet stem was cooler than the middle, the first hammer blows upset the stem, squashed it to fill the hole. By that time, the heat had crept back to the end of the stem and, with alternate hammer blows, the two riveters formed the head.

An experienced crew took about 2 ½ minutes to hand drive a rivet. Multiply that by the hundreds of thousands, if not millions, of rivets required for a large bridge, and you'll begin to get a sense of the intense work necessary to build those early steel bridges. Hand riveting was very hard work, "the hardest manual labor," according to one source, and became harder and harder as larger, thicker plates were used. But riveters were among the highest paid skilled workers.

Now that they were skilled riveters, the Kanien'kéhaka were in even greater demand. After completing the Canadian Pacific Railway bridge at Kahnawake (1886), the Dominion Bridge Company began work on the Sault Sainte Marie International Railroad Bridge (locally called the Soo Bridge) in northern Michigan, spanning two canals and a river to connect the twin cities of Sault Sainte Marie, Michigan, and Sault Sainte Marie, Ontario. Kanien'kéhaka riveting gangs went straight to the Soo Bridge, and more than fifty of them were up in the trusses. One of these men, years later, recalled a new development on this bridge. "The Indian boys turned the Soo Bridge into a college for themselves. The way they worked it, as soon as one apprentice was trained, they'd send back to the reservation for another one. By and by, there'd be enough for a new Indian gang. When the new gang was organized, there'd be a shuffle-up—a couple of men from the old gangs would go into the new gang and a couple of the new men would go into the old gangs; the old would balance the new." Soon there were over seventy skilled Kanien'kéhaka bridgemen on the job. It was from this bridge that Joe Diabo fell to his death, the first Kanien'kéhaka ironworker casualty.

Ironwork was a dangerous job. More ironworkers were killed or injured on the job than in any other construction trade. There were neither unions nor safety regulations to look after the workers' interests. They wore overalls, worked shirtless in hot weather, and wouldn't think of wearing gloves. Foremen could be distinguished by their white shirts and ties, and derby hats. Hardhats, steel-toe shoes, and safety harnesses and nets were still half a century away.

The ironworkers accepted the risks as a part of life. The custom among the Kanien'kéhaka was never to say a man "died" on the job, but to say he "fell." Early bridgemen had a saying that an ironworker never ages; he is always killed before he grows old. The danger was what attracted the Kanien'kéhaka to the job, and few would think of doing anything else. Living right on the edge of life and death as they did, ironworkers in the old days had quite a reputation for being rowdy, earning them the name "Cowboys of the Sky."

One of two steel crosses at the village of Kahnawake commemorating Mohawk ironworkers killed on the job.

"Mohawk ironworkers know what they like about the job. It is the thrill of doing something that most people couldn't and doing it better than those that try. Each steel skyscraper and expansive bridge is testimony to the Indian spirit to survive, to seek, and to achieve."
–Richard Hill, Six Nations

After watching Montreal profit from the Victoria Bridge, the business people of Quebec City wanted their own bridge over the St. Lawrence. The St. Lawrence is a wide river between the Great Lakes and the Atlantic traveled by huge ore boats and tankers hundreds of feet long. Below Montreal, the river is almost two miles wide. At Quebec, it narrows to less than a mile. The high escarpments on both banks would make it easier to build a bridge high enough to allow huge oceangoing ships to pass underneath.

But the river also presented some serious challenges to bridge engineers. The water is deep there, almost 200 feet deep out in the middle of the river, and the currents are strong. This, added to the large number of ships on the river, ruled out any possibility of piers in midstream. The tides rise and fall 18 feet, and during severe winters, the ice jams in the narrows can pile up to 50 feet. Massive mid-channel masonry bridge piers, even if they could be sunk in the deep, fast-flowing waters, would create unacceptable hazards for shipping. All together, the conditions facing engineers at Quebec would require a structure bigger and more difficult to build than any bridge in the world.

Ironworkers lift a bundle of eyebars into place, beginning work on the south anchor arm of the Quebec Bridge.

But with the development of Bessemer steel, the impossible bridge at Quebec became possible.

Now that engineers had the material they needed, the next question was what kind of bridge was best suited to the difficult conditions at Quebec? The answer to that question was found in Scotland. The railroad bridge over the Firth of Forth, built in 1890 and still in use today, has an incredible clear span of 1,700 feet. The immense trusses, 330 feet deep, made of steel tubes and a web of girders appear to spring across the river in three great leaps. It was in its time the most impressive bridge in the world and still attracts visitors today. The Firth of Forth Bridge was an inspiration to American engineers.

A bridge design like the Firth of Forth would be one of the contenders for a new long-span bridge across the St. Lawrence River at Quebec. The conditions were similar. The bridge at Quebec would require a 1,800-foot clear span soaring 150 feet above the water, making it the largest bridge in North America, with the longest span anywhere in the world. The deck would be wide enough for two railroad tracks, two trolley tracks, and two roadways. On each side, outside the trusses, would be walkways.

The man chosen to oversee the project was an American engineer, Theodore Cooper. He would be responsible for designing the bridge and overseeing its construction. Though famed as a structural engineer, Cooper had never designed or built anything as big as a major bridge, certainly nothing of the size and complexity of the project he was about to undertake. He admired the work of James Eads, who had completed the first bridge over the Misssissippi in 1874, and wanted to be regarded as a great bridge builder like him. The bridge at Quebec would be the crowning achievement of his long career.

The contract for the design of the bridge, fabrication of the components, and construction was awarded to the Phoenix Bridge Company of Phoenixville, Pennsylvania. Phoenix was one of the leading bridge design, fabrication, and construction firms of the century. However, they had had problems with some still unsolved mysteries of bridge design. In recent years, they had experienced four serious, spectacular failures resulting in trusses dropping into the river and collapsing under trains, altogether taking twenty-three lives. Oddly, none of this seemed to matter when Phoenix was chosen. All eyes were on the Quebec Bridge, with its 1,800-foot channel span, 100 feet longer than the Firth of Forth

Bridge. "Quebec will have the honor to possess the largest bridge span in the world," the president of the bridge board boasted, "which will be the most marvelous feat of engineering which any country can show."

THE WORK BEGINS

Work on the bridge began on October 2, 1900, with the construction of the two south masonry piers. Because of money problems and labor disputes, the ironwork would not begin until four years later. When the ironwork finally got underway, sixty men from Kahnawake traveled 140 miles down the river to sign on with the Phoenix Bridge Company. The Kanien'kéhaka were excited about working on the new bridge, welcoming the challenges presented by its unprecedented size. A punk (an apprentice) recalled many years later: "We all wanted to work the Quebec Bridge job because they had so much trouble with it. We wanted to show them that we could build it, even if nobody else could." They worked eleven-hour days, six days a week.

Inevitably, such a huge project would present some problems. In reviewing the plans, the Canadian Government's Chief Engineer of Railways and Canals found fault with Cooper's calculations of the stresses on the bridge. The problem went back to the beginning of the design process when Cooper had changed the channel span from 1,600 to 1,800 feet. The Chief Engineer recommended a bridge engineer be appointed to review the plans, but Cooper objected vehemently, protesting, "This puts me in the position of a subordinate, which I cannot accept. There is nobody competent to criticize us." The Chief Engineer reluctantly gave in, and Cooper was allowed full responsibility for all technical decisions.

There are at least three kinds of stresses operating on a bridge. There are the stresses caused by the bridge's own weight, what engineers call the "dead load." Added to this are the stresses caused by the "live load" on the bridge, in this case the trains, trolleys, automobiles, and pedestrians moving across the span. And then there are stresses caused by wind pressure pushing against the sides of the trusses. Early on, engineers ignored, miscalculated, or underestimated stresses of wind, and bridges actually blew down.

The small traveler erecting the south end of the cantilever span, August 15, 1907.

When Cooper calculated the dead load of the bridge, he came up with 6,659 tons for each anchor arm and 6,603 tons for each cantilever arm. Then, several years later, as the south anchor arm was completed and the cantilever arm begun, engineers at Phoenix made an alarming discovery. In changing the channel span from 1,600 to 1,800 feet, they had neglected to recalculate the dead load! The actual weight of the anchor arms was over 9,000 tons—an error of almost 2,400 tons. The weight of the entire bridge, originally estimated at 31,400 tons, would actually be 38,800 tons. To correct the error, the steel erected so far would have to be torn down, all the parts resized, and construction started over again. Still confident his calculations were correct, however, Cooper insisted that the weights were well within the limits of safety. Work on the bridge continued.

When the 1907 construction season began—work stopped from November until the onset of spring—the enormous trusses loomed above the river, held together by 150,000 rivets. At this point in a cantilever's construction, care

One of the huge bottom chord sections for the anchor arm is lifted off flatcars by the big traveler.

Taken on August 28, this is possibly the last photograph of the Quebec bridge before its collapse late the next afternoon. Despite orders to stop work, the little traveler had been moved out to the end ready to begin erection of the next panel. Behind is the heavy large traveler.

This photo of the south cantilever arm, taken from the large traveler on the anchor arm, shows how the top chord is made up of bundles of eyebars.

must be taken to preserve a delicate balance between the weight of the cantilever and anchor arms. As the name suggests, the thousands of tons of steel reaching out over the river cantilever out, hanging from the anchor arm. Added to all the dead weight of the cantilever arm are two traveler cranes that lift the girders and beams into place. There is also a steam locomotive moving back and forth from the bank to the end of the bridge, bringing flat cars loaded with steel out to the cranes. Even the amount of steel brought out to the end of the bridge must be carefully calculated and watched so as not to unbalance the whole structure.

It was at this stage that the erecting crew first became aware of a problem with the bottom chord—the heavy steel girders running the length of the bridge along the bottom. Think of the immense weight of the cantilever arm and the way it "hangs" from the anchor arm. The top chord is being stretched, downward, and is in tension. The bottom chord is being squeezed against the main pier supporting the bridge, and, therefore, is under compression. What the engineers saw was the bottom chord on the left side buckling, crumpling under the 30 tons of compressive forces acting on it. The ironworkers, too, noticed that the sections of the chord were not coming together as they should have. The holes for the rivets were out of alignment by as much as ¼ inch, and the riveters were unable to rivet the sections of the bottom chord together. When apprised of the situation, Cooper, who remained in New York and hadn't actually seen the problem, replied, "Make as good work of it as you can. It is not serious."

A month later, in early August, an engineer at the site, Norman McClure, noticed the misalignment in other chord members. Suggestions for correcting the problem flew back and forth between McClure and Cooper in New York. Cooper dismissed the idea that the chord members were buckling under the load, concluding that they came that way from the shop. How was it, McClure asked, that they hadn't noticed it before? "One thing I am reasonably sure of," he wrote to Cooper, "and that is that the bend has occurred since the chord has been under stress, and was not present when the chord was placed."

Cooper clung to his theory that the chord members had somehow been damaged. "These chords have been hit by those suspended beams used during the erection," he wrote to McClure, "while they were being put in place or taken down." McClure replied: "I have personally examined every member yet erected in this bridge. If these ribs then had been this much out of line before erecting, it would be well nigh impossible to miss seeing them." The situation, as observed by engineers and workers on the bridge, began to change almost daily.

COUNTDOWN TO DISASTER

August 20. Two weeks have now gone by since the problem was discovered. A Quebec Bridge & Railway Company inspector finds that three more girders on the right side of the bridge are bent. Over the next few days, he revisits the chord and notes that the distortion is getting worse.

August 23. The engineers discover that two more chord members on the right side of the cantilever arm have pulled ½ inch out of alignment. Another bend is discovered, this one on the left side of the anchor arm.

August 27. The bend in the anchor arm is worse. The engineers, inspectors, and erection foreman meet, inspect the chord carefully, and measure the amount of bending. A week ago, the chord member was ¾ inch out of line. It is now 2 ¼ inches out of line. It is even worse than that. The chords are beginning to twist into reverse curves. Once again they ask the inspector at the storage yard, and once again he confirms that the chord members were straight when they left the yard. And still, the engineers refuse to accept the obvious—the bridge is failing. They discuss the possibility of one of them going to New York to ask Cooper for advice. But that idea is dismissed. No one wants to confront Cooper with the facts. After all, Theodore Cooper is one of the most renowned and respected engineers in the world. Instead, McClure sends a letter to Cooper explaining the situation and his decision to stop work on the bridge until they hear back from him. McClure calls the men off the bridge.

August 28. Everyone waits anxiously for an answer from New York. Not a word is let out to the workers. But, of course, they know. A riveting gang noticed the bends, word spread, and now every man on the bridge knows something is up. Disregarding McClure's orders, the foreman sends the men back out onto the bridge. As he explains later, "the moral effect of holding up the work would be very bad on all concerned and might also stop the work for this season on account of losing the men."

Unaware that work has resumed and the men are out on the bridge, the engineers continue discussions about how the chords might be repaired. Still, with all that has happened over the last few days, they tell themselves over and over that the chord members must have been dropped somehow in the yard or poorly assembled in the Phoenix shops. As engineer William D. Middleton put it in his engrossing book on the bridge: "No one was able to see that the unthinkable was happening. The Quebec Bridge was slowly beginning to collapse."

But the men on the bridge know the situation has become dangerous. Several men have stayed away from work. They noticed the engineers, foremen, and inspectors conferring, gathering in little groups, going here, going there. Some, no doubt, saw the concern on their faces, maybe even overheard their deliberations. Talk of the situation spreads among the men. At the end of the day, many of them climb down to the bottom chord to see what is happening. They know what the engineers and inspectors refuse to admit; the steel wasn't twisted and buckled like that when they put it in place and riveted the splices.

The men working on the bridge are more aware than the engineers of what is happening to the bottom chord—and more worried. They, too, decide to perform an experiment. D. B. Haley, president of the union local, knows what he is looking at. "I found that it was bulging out on both sides." he later reported. "The inside web was bending toward Montreal and the outside was bending toward Quebec, showing there was too much compression put on and it would not stand the strain and it was giving. We put a mark on the bulge and decided to visit it the following evening and see if the deflections were increasing any." One of the bridgemen later recalled talking with a group of Kanien'kéhaka riveters. "They said there was a place in the chord. I do not know whereabouts, where it was bent, and they were trying to jack it together, and they could not jack the plates together and riveted it up the way it was."

August 29

11:00 A.M. Theodore Cooper arrives at his office to find McClure waiting for him. Alarmed by McClure's description of the situation on the bridge, he immediately sends a telegram to Phoenix: "Add no more load to the bridge until after consideration of the facts." For some unexplainable reason, Cooper thinks he will get faster results if he wires the bridge company instead of the bridge. Neither of them knows that work has resumed on the bridge, and that a 200-ton traveler crane has been moved all the way out to the end of the span. McClure decides to telegraph Cooper's decision to the bridge site as well—but, in his haste to get to Phoenixville, he forgets!

1:15 P.M. Cooper's telegram is placed on the desk of John Stewart Deans, Phoenix's chief engineer. But Deans is away for the day. (Deans's secretary later acknowledges seeing the letter on the desk, but says "comparatively little importance was attached to it.")

3:00 P.M. Deans returns to his office, reads the telegram, but takes no action, deciding to wait until McClure arrives from New York.

5:15 P.M. McClure arrives in Deans's office, and they decide not to act on Cooper's instruction until the next morning.

TIME SEEMED TO STOP

August 29

5:15 P.M. As McClure and Deans discuss the situation, the workday on the bridge is coming to an end. A locomotive pushing two flatcar loads of steel chugs slowly onto the bridge, headed for the traveler at the far end of the cantilever arm.

5:30 P.M. "Everything was going ok when suddenly I could hear the sounds of the rivet heads shearing and popping like gun fire," Kanien'kéhaka John Montour later recalls. "Then there was this tremor like an earthquake and a roar. Then this bad grinding sound and a thunder as the bridge fell into the water." Montour survives because, as the punk of his riveting gang, he has been sent off the bridge to buy food. Frozen in fear, he cannot see the bridge from where he stands. He can only imagine what has happened.

What Montour heard was 19,000 tons of steel, the entire south half of the bridge, falling into the river. Some survivors don't recall hearing anything, just the strange feel of the bridge falling away from under them. D. B. Haley later said: "I was on the extreme end of it and the first thing I knew I caught myself going through the air. I realized that the iron fell very much faster than I did

The wreckage the day after the bridge's collapse. Taken from about the same vantage point as the photograph on page 40.

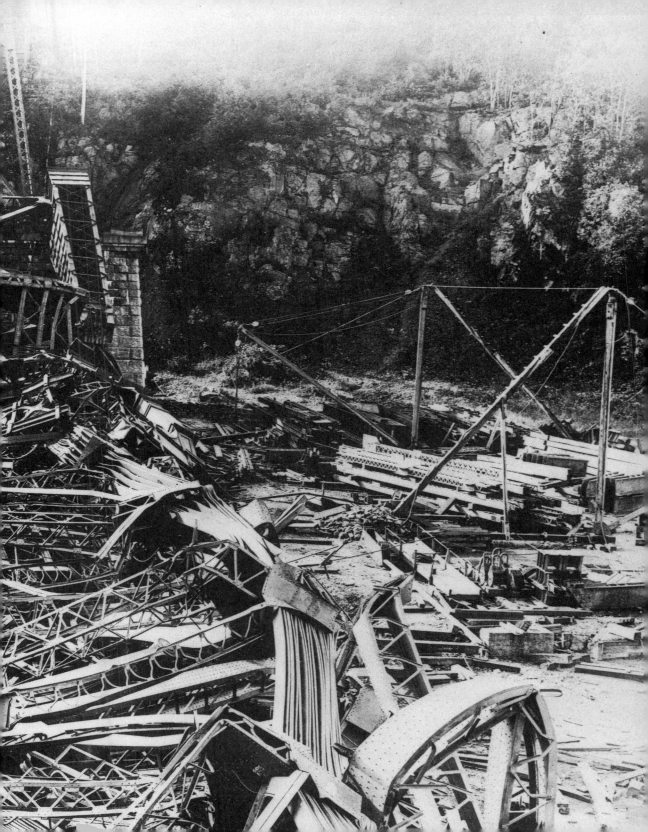

and left me falling through the air. The next thing I remember I was deep in water."

One witness described the sound as like "a clap of thunder." *The New York Times* described the final moments of the Quebec Bridge this way: "Time seemed to stop indefinitely as thousands of tons began to descend. Amidst the pitiful cries of the doomed men, everything came crashing down three hundred feet to the water below. A mighty earthquake upheaval was heard for miles around as steel, timber, and concrete met the dark water. Then, a long, eerie silence settled upon the tragic scene broken only by a few mournful echoes of pain and the torment of men slipping into death."

Of the eighty-six men who were on the structure when it collapsed, only eleven survived. Among the dead was fourteen-year-old Stanley Wilson, who worked as a water boy for ten cents an hour. Thirty-eight Kanien'kéhaka were on the bridge when it collapsed; only five survived, two of them injured.

As news of the disaster spreads, thousands of curious onlookers arrive on the scene. The anchor arm lies on the beach.

Kahnawake bridgeman Alexander Beauvais later told his incredible story to the Royal Commission investigating the tragedy. About half an hour before the bridge fell, he found the broken-off heads of two rivets. "While I was driving two or three other rivets after that, I found the first one broken off. There is another one broken," he said to himself, wondering why the rivets were breaking almost as fast as he finished them. "I tested it with a drift pin and it was broken off straight. You could turn the one end and the other end would be still. I called Mr. Meredith, the rivet boss, and also to see that the ribs were bending in. He looked down there and told me that it was not any worse than the others. He did not think it serious."

Asked what chord he was in, Beauvais replied, "No. 10, Montreal [left] side. I was driving rivets, and I was about to shoot another rivet when the crash came down. I was right inside the chord. When this chord landed it did not land on the ground. It stood three or four feet in the air. I held on to the chord and never touched the ground. As soon as everything was still, I came out. It was easy to stay there because I was tight in there. I had one leg broken and my nose was broken."

Meanwhile young John Montour, away from the bridge to buy food for his gang, realized what had happened. "I didn't know what to do. I had to find out how many people from the town were hurt, but they wouldn't let us near the site. Everybody in my crew died, including my mother's brother, my brother, and cousin. It was bad. I knew I had to find another Indian. I finally met Joe Regis and we went to find a phone to call town." In Kahnawake there was only one telephone, in the post office, where the postmaster received the first call at about 6:30 p.m. The news traveled from person to person through the town, and soon a crowd stood around the post office, remaining throughout the night, waiting for news of a son, father, cousin, uncle, husband, brother, or friend. Almost everyone in Kahnawake had lost someone close.

Rescuers arriving at the scene stood around helpless. Most of the men had died instantly, crushed under the tangle of steel. But many were trapped alive in the wreckage. "Their groans could be heard by the anxious crowds waiting at the water's edge," *The New York Times* reported, "but nothing so far can be done to rescue them or relieve their sufferings. There are no searchlights available, and by the feeble light of the lanterns it is impossible to even locate some of the sufferers." There was no heavy equipment or cutting torches to free the injured and dying men from the mass of twisted steel. The priest of the nearby Silley parish, Father A. E. McGuire, was one of the first to arrive on the scene, descending by rope down the cliff face, wading out into the water, clambering over the wreckage, stopping here and there to administer last rites to each of the trapped men. Around six o'clock that evening, the river level began to rise with the incoming tide. Eventually it reached 13 feet, silencing, one by one, the victims' moans and cries for help.

By the next morning, the full impact of the disaster hit Kahnawake. A group of men and women traveled downriver to the bridge site to claim the dead. They returned the next day with only eight bodies, all that had been found.

In the bridge's collapse, twenty-four Kanien'kéhaka women were widowed and fifty-six children left fatherless. Few would receive any compensation for their losses. Among the dead were seven members of the Daillebout family—four sons, an uncle, a cousin, and a brother-in-law; three men from the Deer family; two from the Mitchell; and two from the Jocks families. Joseph Daillebout left behind nine children, five boys and four girls, ranging in age from nineteen to two, several of whom had not yet been named. His wife was pregnant, and she had no insurance except a $100 death benefit from the union. But Kahnawake took care of its own. Several of the widows had nothing from the union, no life insurance, but still replied to the Indian Agent's survey that they were "in no need." The Canadian government appointed an Indian Agent as guardian of the children who had lost their fathers, and made a payment of $100,000 in their names.

A few days after the bridge's collapse, a funeral was held for the eight men whose bodies now lay in simple wooden coffins before the altar of a little stone church by the river. The church choir sang in Mohawk. The archbishop of Montreal, Louis Joseph Napoleon Paul Bruchesi said mass. "I am here to pray and share your grief," he began, as a priest who ministered to the Kanien'kéhaka translated the archbishop's sermon into Mohawk.

Most everyone in the community was there, accompanying the bodies to the churchyard cemetery. The mourners joined two Iroquois singers offering up a song of the dead as the coffins were laid in a common grave. Men and boys, whose kin now lay in the ground, stepped forward with shovels, breaking the

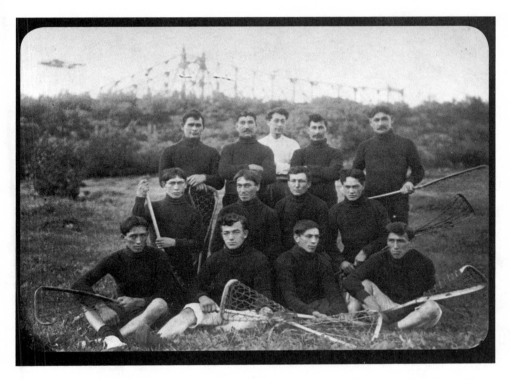

The Kahnawake lacrosse team, all of whom were working on the bridge, posed for this team photograph with the bridge in the background just a few days before the disaster. Eight of the team members were killed and one seriously injured.

mournful hush as clumps of soil drummed on the wooden coffins below. As the weeks passed, the river gave up more of the dead, and the bodies of four more ironworkers were brought back to Kahnawake. Forty remain with the wreckage to this day.

JUDGMENT

In the days immediately following the disaster, the companies began covering their tracks. A flurry of letters went back and forth as each man attempted to "correct a misstatement," explain what he really said, or make clear "this is what

I really meant." Rather than accept any responsibility, engineers, inspectors, and Phoenix Bridge Company officials all accused one another, distancing themselves from what happened. Cooper pointed his finger at Phoenix, saying they were guilty of poor workmanship, and at the engineers, both at Phoenix and on the bridge, whom he regarded as being unqualified. Never mind that Cooper had hired and worked for years with these very same people. Never mind that Cooper had refused to have his work reviewed by the government's Chief Engineer of Railways and Canals who saw problems in the design from the very beginning. Never mind that he had never actually been at the construction site and never troubled himself to go look at the failing girders.

The Canadian government immediately appointed a Royal Commission of prominent engineers to investigate what had happened at the Quebec Bridge and why. But as an editorial in *Scientific American* made clear, there was a bigger issue: "The tremendous significance of this disaster lies in the suspicion, which to-day is staring every engineer coldly in the face, that there is something wrong with our theories of bridge design, at least as applied to a structure of the size of the Quebec Bridge."

To the credit of the Royal Commission, they did their homework and they did it well. Ignoring Cooper's conflicting testimony, the Commission was determined to find out for themselves what actually happened. Compression tests were made on a one-third-scale model of the lower chord in the anchor arm, the member that had failed. Every detail of the full-sized girder was carefully copied in the model. When the test loading reached the critical level, the latticing crumpled, and the rivets sheared off with "explosive violence." So essential was this one girder to the whole structure that its failure caused everything else in the bridge to fail.

Despite the finger-pointing, it became clear to the Commission that Cooper alone was responsible for the design of the failed bridge. David Reeves, president of the Phoenix Bridge Company, testified that Cooper had refused to make any changes after problems were called to his attention. "Mr. Cooper," he told the Commission, "made modifications to the unit-stresses to be employed on the

Plaque commemorating the 31 Mohawk bridgemen killed in the collapse of the bridge.

various members which very much increased them beyond any precedent, and by so doing placed the whole design in a field outside the benefit of experience. The fall of the bridge is to be laid directly to the change in the unit-stresses as made by Mr. Cooper."

Neither did the Royal Commission pull their punches. In fact, they concluded, Cooper had exceeded the stress limits by as much as 24 percent. Not only were the beams and girders undersized, the Commission concluded, they were also inadequately connected. Cooper was also faulted for using too low a value for the dead load. In short, there was not enough metal in the bridge. "This error," the Commission concluded, "was of sufficient magnitude to have required condemnation of the bridge."

The blame was placed squarely on Phoenix's chief design engineer, Peter Szlapka—who also had never visited the bridge—and Theodore Cooper, whose "erroneous assumptions . . . tended to hasten the disaster." The report of the Royal Commission fills a heavy volume, but its conclusions come down to a few words:

- The design of the chords that failed was made by Mr. P. L. Szlapka, the designing engineer of the Phoenix Bridge Company.
- The design was examined and officially approved by Mr. Theodore Cooper, consulting engineer of the Quebec Bridge & Railway Company.
- The failure cannot be attributed directly to any cause other than errors in judgment on the part of these two engineers.
- The loss of life on August 29, 1907, might have been prevented by the exercise of better judgment on the part of those in responsible charge of the work for the Quebec Bridge & Railway Company and for the Phoenix Bridge Company.

Theodore Cooper's reputation and career was wrecked. He retired from engineering, never again to design another structure. But a lesson had been learned. As structural engineer William D. Middleton explains, "Within the engineering community at large, the disaster brought a realization that engineers did not know as much as they thought they did about the design and behavior of extremely large and heavily loaded compression members. The large-scale testing, experimentation and study that followed the disaster all helped to develop a more scientific basis for the analysis and design of large compression members and their connections that significantly advanced the art of design for a new generation of major bridges that followed."

For the grieving families at Kahnawake, the Commission's findings were cold comfort, if they were noticed at all. The lives of the Kanien'kéhaka had been forever altered.

One of the steel finials that once topped the south portal of the bridge marks the common grave of the 76 bridgemen from the village of Saint-Romuald who were killed on the bridge.

BOOMING OUT

"The sky dome is our roof, and the earth is our mother. Anywhere we go, it's still our home, and it belongs to us, even though governments separate us by borders, states, and fences. These are foreign concepts to us. The bones of our ancestors are under our feet."
—Jerry McDonald, Mohawk ironworker

Despite the devastating loss of life and unimaginable grief visited on Kahnawake families, the men's enthusiasm for working on high steel was not dampened. It was just the opposite. The bridgemen at Quebec had died an honorable death, a warrior's death—a purposeful, meaningful death—because they died doing what they wanted to do, because they died providing a good life for their families. Little boys still dreamed of the day when they could be ironworkers—many later recalled lying about their age so they could work at fourteen or fifteen—and the young men joined up in riveting and erecting gangs in even greater numbers. They returned to build the new, redesigned bridge at Quebec, eventually completed in 1917.

It's hard for those of us who prefer to live our lives on the ground to understand this work. Mike Phillips, a retired connector (the most dangerous job of all), whose tired body reflects decades of work on bridges and skyscrapers, explains the lure of high steel this way: "I walked in places where nobody walked before. I dream about it sometimes. I dream about how free I was. If you are a

Mohawk ironworkers on the Hell Gate Bridge.

connector on a bridge, you are one of the first ones to walk across the river. Can you imagine being that happy? I see myself doing a dance on the steel."

There would, however, be some new rules. The women, coming together in council, made the men promise they would not all work together on the same project. Over half of Kahnawake's high steel workers had been on the Quebec Bridge. When another bridge being built over the St. Lawrence, at Cornwall Island, collapsed, killing several men from another Mohawk community at Akwesasne, the women of that community also insisted that the men spread out in smaller groups. The possibilities of death and injury are facts of life for anyone who walks high steel, but never again would so many husbands, fathers, brothers, uncles, and grandfathers be taken at one time.

Events of the time seemed to support the women's decision. A construction boom in Canada and America made it possible for the Mohawks to work on any number of projects, opening a new chapter in their story. The men, not only of Kahnawake, but from Akwesasne and other Iroquois towns began "booming out."

The reputation of the Mohawk ironworkers had become almost legend in the construction trades. These most skilled of workers were welcome on any project, and they had no difficulty finding work. When they ran out of bridges to build, the Mohawks worked on other kinds of steel construction—factories, powerhouses, railroad stations, grain elevators, department stores, hotels, apartment houses, wharfs, hospitals. Any steel structure going up in Canada had Mohawks on it. When there wasn't enough to do in Canada, they crossed the border to work on jobs in Buffalo, Cleveland, and Detroit. Conway Jocks describes what happened next.

> Paul Diabo was a pivotal character in the history of Mohawk ironworking. He began traveling to the U.S. as an ironworker in 1912, working mostly in New York City along with a growing number of Mohawks who had gone to New York to find work on the future Woolworth building and the bridges linking Manhattan to the Bronx. Think of them as latter-day war parties and fur traders, bringing home the booty in the form of paychecks.
>
> By the middle 1920s there were three riveting gangs in New York

. . . Most of the Indian ironworkers could hardly speak English, which was okay because the Indian gangs communicated with each other in Mohawk, and also there is an elaborate system of hand signals. Eventually the men learned English and when they returned home they were quick to show it off, which encouraged the learning of that language—English with a blend of Mohawk and Brooklyn accents.

One of the first large projects to attract Mohawks to New York City was the Hell Gate Bridge. A long-span bridge over the East River, the Hell Gate was a fitting symbol of the new Mohawk bridgemen. It was, first of all, designed by one of the most famous engineers of the day, Gustav Lindenthal, who envisioned the massive, soaring arch as a gateway to the country's foremost city. Designed to carry four railroad tracks over a clear span of 1,017 feet, it was the heaviest bridge in the world, weighing 2,000 tons carrying an unheard of load of 76,000 pounds per linear foot. To accomplish this, Lindenthal called for four of the biggest steel members ever assembled, weighing 185 tons apiece, made up of steel plates two inches thick. The girders were so large that bridgemen could walk around inside of them with ease. Riveters had their work cut out for them. Fastening the bridge together are 1,174,000 of the largest rivets—1 ¼ inches in diameter and up to 11 inches long—ever used on any engineering project. Because of the tides, the bridge had to be built in two sections cantilevered out over the river. When the two sections of the bridge met in the middle, in 1916, the distance between them was exactly what the engineers had calculated—5/16 of an inch!

Within a few years, gangs of Mohawk ironworkers were booming out all over North America, helping build Chicago, New York, Detroit, Philadelphia, and Toronto. As Conway Jocks points out, the long absences required of this new life was not unlike the life the Mohawks had lived for centuries. The men had always left the village for months, to canoe and trap in the far-away backwoods of Canada or to war against distant tribes. And because of the matriarchal structure of Mohawk settlements, life in the village went on without interruption. While the men were away, the women cared for the children, cultivated the fields, harvested their crops, and performed the necessary rituals and ceremonies. Of

Hell Gate Bridge, completed in 1916, provided a railroad connection between Queens and the Bronx over the East River.

course, not all of the men were away. Some continued in their traditional role as hunters and helped the women with their chores.

VOYAGEURS AGAIN

Look at a map of New York City and find Broadway, running the full length of Manhattan Island. Follow Broadway north as it becomes Route 9, north until the commotion of city streets gives way to the quiet of the Hudson River valley, north as the little two-lane road passes through Rhinebeck, Hudson, Albany, across the Mohawk River, north until it begins to climb up into the foothills and cool, dark pine forests of the Adirondack Mountains.

For over a hundred miles, Route 9 winds through the dense forest, opening now and then to grand views of Mount Marcy (5,344 feet) and Big Slide Mountain (4,255 feet). For over a hundred miles, you are traveling along the eastern boundary of the Mohawk's ancestral lands. For centuries the Mohawk fished the thousands of miles of rivers and streams and more than 2,000 lakes and ponds of Kanienke. They traveled easily over the deep snows of winter on snowshoes fashioned of bent wood and strips of hide. This is the land of James Fenimore Cooper's *Leatherstocking Tales,* the land of Chingachgook and Uncas, *The Last of the Mohicans.* Descending out of the mountains, the road runs along the west bank of Lake Champlain, across the Canadian border to Kahnawake.

In a few seconds you have traced the four-hundred-mile journey home made by hundreds of Mohawk ironworkers, the new voyageurs, every Friday night for decades. You have to imagine driving all this way after a day of muscle-wrenching, bone-crushing work. Author Gay Talese accompanied ironworker Danny Montour and two other Mohawks on one of these harrowing Friday night races to Kahnawake.

> Only once during the trip did Montour stop; in Malden, New
> York, he stopped at a Hot Shoppe for ten minutes to get a cup
> of coffee—and there he saw Mike Tarbell and several other

Indians also bound for Canada. By 11 PM, he was speeding past Warrensburg, New York, and an hour or so later he pulled off the expressway and was on Route 9, a two-lane back road, and Stacey was yelling, "Only forty miles more to go, Danny-boy."

Now, with no radar and no cars coming or going, Danny Montour's big Buick was blazing along at 120 miles per hour, swishing past the tips of trees, skimming over the black road—and it seemed, at any second, that a big truck would surely appear in the windshield, as trucks always appear, suddenly, in motion-picture films to demolish a few actors near the end of the script.

But, on this particular night, there were no trucks for Danny Montour.

At 1:35 AM, he took a sharp turn onto a long dirt road, then sped past a large black bridge that was silhouetted in the moonlight over the St. Lawrence Seaway—it was the Canadian railroad bridge that had been built in 1886, the one that got Indians started as ironworkers. With a screech of his brakes, Montour stopped in front of a white house.

"We're home, you lucky Indians," he yelled. The Indian in the back seat who had been sleeping at this time, woke up, blinked. Then the lights went on in the white house; it was Montour's house, and everybody went in for a quick drink, and soon Danny's wife, Lorraine, was downstairs, and so was the two-year-old boy, Mark. Outside, other horns were honking, other lights burned; and they remained alive, some of them, until 4AM Then, one by one, they went out, and the last of the Indians fell asleep.

After a cherished couple of days with their families and, perhaps, a Sunday afternoon game of lacrosse or hockey, the men would pile back into their cars and drive south for eleven or twelve hours, arriving back in Manhattan in time to begin a full day's work on high steel. When Interstate 87 was completed in the 1960s, the driving time between Kahnawake and New York was cut in half, but the sadness of Sunday evenings remained. Gay Talese continues, describing the trip back.

> Then, anywhere from 8 PM to 11 PM, the big cars filled with ironworkers will begin to rumble down the reservation's roads, and then toward the routes to the expressway back to New York. It is a sad time for Indian women, these Sunday evenings, and the ride back to New York seems twice as long to the men as did the Friday-night ride coming up.
>
> And so on this Sunday evening, Danny Montour kissed his wife goodbye, and hugged his son, and then went to pick up the others for the long ride back.
>
> "Now be careful," Lorraine said from the porch.
>
> "Don't worry," he said.
>
> And all day Monday she, and other Indian women, half-waited for the phone calls, hoping they would never come. And when they did not come this particular Monday, the women were happy, and by midweek the happiness would grow into a blithe anticipation of what was ahead—the late-Friday sounds of the horns, the croaking call of Cadillacs, and Buicks, and Oldsmobiles, the sounds that would bring their husbands home . . . and will take their sons away.

DOWNTOWN KAHNAWAKE

At the turn of century, New York was the largest, richest, and fastest growing city in the country. Land on Manhattan Island was limited, so while other cities could grow outward, New York had to grow upward. And though the skyscraper was invented in Chicago, the city had passed an ordinance in 1893 limiting the height of buildings to ten stories. In New York, however, the sky was the limit. What's more, as city workers began to move to the communities across the

Hudson, Harlem, and East Rivers, New Yorkers would need bridges, many long bridges, to get to and from work each day.

By the 1920s, Kahnawake ironworkers began to realize that there was enough work in New York to keep them there for years. More and more of the young men had come down to the City, following their fathers, brothers, and uncles onto the high steel. The pay was good; at a time when factory workers earned about $8.50 a week, ironworkers were getting $4 a day. They joined the Brooklyn local of the newly chartered Bridge, Structural, and Ornamental Iron Workers Union. And some of them stayed.

Since the union hall was where they were assigned to jobs and "shaped up" into gangs, the men took furnished rooms in the neighborhood. A whole gang (four people) would rent a 2 ½ room apartment. It wasn't long before some of the men gave up the long, harrowing drives to Kahnawake and back, the hurried few hours with their families, and the sad Sunday goodbyes, and brought their families with them to Brooklyn. Tom Jacobs was one of the very first Kanien'kéhaka to migrate to Brooklyn.

> I got to Brooklyn about 1923 or '24. I can't remember which it was. But I'll always remember my first job here, because it was almost my last. It was a big apartment building uptown in Manhattan, on Fifth Avenue. I was working on a corner 200, maybe 300 feet up. My foot slipped, and all of a sudden there was nothing under me but the ground, so far away I could hardly see it. When I felt myself falling, I stuck out my arm, and it caught a beam. I just hung there, swinging in the wind. When the other men saw me, they all began to shout: "Tom, what are you going to do?" What a question! There was only one thing I *could* do. I got my other hand up on that beam, and then I chinned myself and got a leg over it and climbed up. I sat there for a while, to get my breath, and then I went back to work.

After Tom got settled down in Brooklyn, he wrote letters home telling his friends and relatives that there was plenty of work and to come down and join him. They did, and the migration from Kahnawake to Brooklyn began.

Mohawk ironworkers enjoy a sunny day off in their Brooklyn neighborhood.

Ironworkers also settled in Detroit and Buffalo. They were, for the first time in the history of Native Americans, creating a new class—the urban Indian.

The North Gowanus neighborhood of Brooklyn (now Boerum Hill), which the Mohawks referred to as "the reservation," eventually became home to hundreds of families from Kahnawake and Akwesasne. They all lived within about ten blocks of each other in old red brick and brownstone apartment houses. Everyone knew each other, the residents recall fondly, and you could always borrow a quarter from a neighbor. The population varied with the seasons from about 500 in October through May to a hundred in midsummer, when families returned to the reserves in Canada.

Brooklyn became home in many ways. Some Mohawks were able to buy apartment buildings and boarding houses, and rent to other Kanien'kéhaka. They owned several of the businesses in the neighborhood, including grocery stores and bars. Bars were important gathering places in the community. They served as a home away from home, where the men picked up telephone messages and mail from family, caught rides back to the reservation, cashed their paychecks, and reconnected with old friends who worked on other jobs. Newly arrived ironworkers would stop by to learn about the community—where there were rooms for rent, where to look for jobs, directions to here and there.

The Wigwam was one of the oldest saloons in Brooklyn, and one of the neighborhood's favorite hangouts. It was owned in those days by a Kahnawake woman, Irene Vilis, and her husband. "Any Indian who was traveling through stopped there," locals would tell you. Irene had grown up in an ironworker's family. She had been one of the children awakened early Saturday mornings to welcome her daddy, and then, with tears in her eyes, watched him drive off Sunday night, not to see him again for a whole week. So she made the men feel at home, served Montreal ale, saw to it that the music they liked was on the jukebox, and gave them a place to wind down from a stressful day. On the walls were painted portraits of Iroquois warriors and chiefs and large framed photographs of the great Sac Indian athlete and Olympian, Jim Thorpe.

Walking into the Wigwam, you could not have guessed what these men did all day. Your first impression would be of a lot of unremarkable-looking men—until you talked to any of them. Then you'd discover remarkable men, like Orvis Diabo sitting in his usual booth. His Mohawk name was Oroniakete, He Carries the Sky, and he was one of the first Kanien'kéhaka ironworkers to move to Brooklyn. His grandfather Miles Diabo was a warwhooper in a Wild West show, one of the last Kahnawake circus Indians. His father, Nazareth Diabo, a pioneer high steel Mohawk, died when the Quebec Bridge collapsed. Orvis started work on a riveting gang when he was nineteen. Thirty-five years of hard work as a heater on bridges and buildings in seventeen states has left him crippled with arthritis and looking much older than he is. "I heated millions of rivets," he said proudly. "When they talk about the men that built this country, one of the men they mean is me."

The Wigwam was also a place to honor fallen ironworkers. On the walls were the hardhats of Indian ironworkers who had fallen to their deaths on the job. When a high steel man fell, a collection was taken up for his family to cover their immediate needs. Stuck in the frame of the mirror behind the bar were notes of thanks from the widows. Over the door hung a sign proclaiming: "the greatest ironworkers in the world pass thru these doors."

The Mohawks referred to Brooklyn as "downtown Kahnawake," and they quickly settled into their new home. A typical family included a husband and wife and a couple of children. Occasionally, households included other family members, usually young women who came down to Brooklyn to work in factories. Except for a few heirlooms brought from the reservation and proudly displayed on the mantel—a drum, masks, rattles, a cradleboard, beadwork, a lacrosse stick—there was little to distinguish Mohawk households from those of their white neighbors. Many of the women spent their spare time making souvenirs— dolls, moccasins, baskets, beadwork handbags, and belts ornamented with ancient Iroquois designs in colored beads. While some brought materials with them from Canada, most got the raw materials they needed for their crafts— beads, deer skin, eagle feathers, leather—from a firm in Manhattan.

Mohawk children, especially, were almost indistinguishable from their Brooklyn neighbors. Most of them attended Public School 47, and the others parochial schools. Joseph Mitchell, a writer who reported on the Mohawks in 1938, found them to be, well, just kids. "Caughnawaga [Kahnawake] children read comic books, listen to the radio while doing their homework, sit twice through double features, and play stick ball in vacant lots the same as other children in the neighborhood; teachers say that they differ mainly in that they are more reserved and polite. They have unusual manual dexterity; by the age of three, most of them are able to tie their shoelaces."

Some of the Mohawks at the time were Roman Catholics. Some had stayed in the old Longhouse religion. Protestants among them found a warm welcome at the Cuyler Presbyterian Church. Perhaps because the congregation included people from many cultures, the Mohawks called it *O-non-sa-to-ken-ti-wa-ten-ros-hens*, the-church-that-makes-friends. The pastor, Rev. Dr. David Munroe Cory, taught himself Mohawk so that he could counsel those who didn't speak English and conduct his service in their language. With the help of one of the women of the congregation, Cory translated the hymnal into Mohawk—a translated version of "Rock of Ages" was among the hymns sung at services—and revised an old Iroquois translation of the Gospel of Luke.

Despite the close-knit neighborhood they had created and the efforts of Reverend Cory, the Mohawks of Brooklyn eventually began to lose their traditional culture. New York and the surrounding boroughs were then, as they are now, a patchwork of ethnic enclaves, making it easy for Mohawk men and women to assimilate. Successive generations of Mohawks became more "American" than Mohawk. Many married non-Indians: Italians, Puerto Ricans, and European Jews who lived in the neighborhood.

Eventually, their children would become strangers to the world of their elders. They no longer spoke their language or knew the history of their people. Alec McComber, an ironworker in the 1950s, recalls that "Most of my coworkers over the years were Kahnawakehronon and our language was heard on the job as well as in the homes, restaurants, and taverns, wherever our people worked. We had a rich vocabulary to describe each job and the many activities involved in the high steel trade—words to describe the riveters, the heaters, and the raising gang were common, but are now rarely used on the job today."

"If the language is lost," lamented another Mohawk, Joseph Deer, "then the culture is lost."

As they grew into adults, Mohawk children in Brooklyn took on ideas about life and values different from the people in Kahnawake, which no longer felt like home. Still, many yearned for the old ways. Orvis Diabo explained his own conflicted feelings this way:

> I feel very low in my mind. I've got to go back to the reservation. I've run out of excuses and I can't put it off much longer. . . . The trouble is, I don't want to go. That is, I do and I don't. I'll try to explain what I mean. An Indian high steel man, when he first leaves the reservation to work in the States, the homesickness just about kills him. The first few years, he goes back as often as he can. . . . After a while he gets married and brings his wife down and starts a family, and he doesn't go back so often. Oh,

he most likely takes his wife and children up for the summer, but he doesn't stay with them. After three or four days, the reservation gets on his nerves and he highballs it back to the States. He gets used to the States.

On the other hand, there's things I look forward to. I look forward to eating real Indian grub again, such as *O-nen-sto*, or corn soup. That's the Mohawk national dish. Some of the women make it down here in Brooklyn, but they use Quaker corn meal. The good old women up on the reservation, they make it the hard way, the way the Mohawks were making it five hundred years ago.

Another thing I look forward to, if I can manage it—I want to attend a longhouse festival. One night, the last time I was home, the longhousers were having a festival. I decided to go up to there. Suddenly the people in the longhouse began to sing and dance and drum on their drums. They were singing Mohawk chants that came down from the old, old red-Indian times. I could hear men's voices and women's voices and children's voices. The Mohawk language, when it's sung, it's beautiful to hear. Oh, it takes your breath away. A feeling ran through me that made me tremble; I had to take a deep breath to quiet my heart, it was beating so fast. I felt very sad; at the same time, I felt very peaceful. I thought I was all alone in the graveyard and then, who loomed up and sat down beside me, but an old high steel man I had been talking to in the store that afternoon. . . . So he said to me, "You're not alone up here. Look over there." I looked where he pointed and I saw a white shirt in among the bushes. And he said, "Look over there," and I saw a cigarette gleaming in the dark. "The bushes are full of Catholics and Protestants," he said. "Every night there's a longhouse festival, they creep up here and listen to the singing. It draws them like flies to honey." So I said, "The longhouse music is beautiful to hear, isn't it?" And he remarked it ought to be, it was the old Indian music.

Truth be told, the women secretly admitted they preferred the fine-ground packaged cornmeal they got in the neighborhood stores to the rough meal ground by their mothers in stone mortars. But, like Orvis, they missed much of reservation life. Whenever Mohawks got together, at church, after the traditional Sunday morning breakfast of fried steak and Indian bread, or at The Wigwam, they sang their traditional songs, always ending with a bittersweet favorite, *Kahnawake tetsitewe,* "Let's Go Back to Kahnawake."

TROUBLE ON THE BORDER

For many families the decision to move to Brooklyn had been forced by growing problems with crossing the Canada/U.S. border. Beginning in the 1920s, United States customs officials began harassing Indians on their way to work. Ironworker Norton Lickers remembered that it often took him four hours to clear customs at the very bridges that he and other Indians had built. But once they reached Brooklyn, the ironworkers' troubles did not end. Immigration agents began forcefully deporting Mohawks back to Canada, declaring that they were "illegal aliens."

Finally, in 1926, the Mohawks decided to fight back. The threat to their livelihoods and homes in the United States was just too great. A meeting of ironworkers was held in New York to discuss what might be done. And they came up with a plan. Ironworker Paul Diabo volunteered to be a test case. He was perfect for the task. He had worked in the United States the longest of any Mohawk, and he spoke Mohawk and English fluently. According to plan, Diabo and his wife left Kahnawake to travel to Philadelphia, where he was working. Soon, as expected, the couple were served with warrants by the Commissioner for Immigration for the Port of Philadelphia and, in March, forcibly returned to Canada.

Once more, the Iroquois skill at organization served them well. The following month, representatives from every Six Nations community in Canada and the United States gathered around the council fire of the Confederacy for a meeting of the Grand Council of the Iroquois, at Onondaga, Michigan.

The representatives discussed the problem. Money would be raised to hire an attorney for Paul Diabo. Because every ironworker had a stake in the outcome, all were asked to contribute a portion of their earnings to the defense fund. A pageant, *Hiawatha the Mohawk*, not performed for years, was dusted off and toured around to raise money.

As the Grand Council's plan unfolded, Paul Diabo returned to Philadelphia with his attorney. He was arrested and charged as an illegal alien.

DEPARTMENT OF IMMIGRATION VS. PAUL K. DIABO

Paul Diabo was tried in the Federal District Court at Trenton, New Jersey. His defense was based on an old precedent in law going back to the Jay Treaty of 1794.

Much of the treaty concerned the U.S./Canada border and protected the rights of British and American citizens living on both sides of it. But it also defined the rights of Indians. Two articles of the treaty were read to the court in defense of Paul Diabo and all of the Mohawk ironworkers. The first stated that neither Canada nor the United States could levy taxes on pelts carried across the border, and specifically stated that Native Americans could not be taxed for carrying goods across the border. The second stated that "it shall at all times to be free to His Majesty's subjects and to the citizens of the United States, and also to the Indians dwelling on either side of the boundary line . . . freely to pass and repass, by land or inland navigation in the respective territories and countries of the two parties."

Attorneys for the Department of Immigration argued that the Jay Treaty had been annulled by the War of 1812 and the Treaty of Ghent, which ended the war. But the judge cited Article 9 of the Treaty of Ghent, in which the United States and Great Britain agreed to "restore to such tribes or nations of Indians all possessions, rights, and privileges which they may have enjoyed, or been entitled to in one thousand eight hundred and eleven, previous to such hostilities."

The Jay Treaty, the justice ruled, was still in effect, protecting the right of Indians to cross the border to hunt or otherwise earn a living without government restrictions. On July 8, 1926, Justice Bodine dismissed the case against Paul Diabo. The Commission appealed its case to a higher court. But Justice John Dickinson upheld the decision of the lower court, explaining:

> The Indians have always been recognized by us as a Nation and as a race independent of our government control. . . . Territorially as a nation they have always been an *imperium to imperio* [a nation within a nation]. The boundary line to establish the respective territory of the United States and Great Britain was clearly not intended to and just as clearly did not affect the Indians. It made no division of their country. From the Indian point of view, he crosses no boundary line. For him, this does not exist.

The Commission appealed the case two more times, eventually reaching the United States Supreme Court. In agreement with the three lower courts, the Supreme Court rejected the Commission's request for a hearing. Once and for all, the courts had affirmed the right of Paul Diabo and future generations of Mohawk ironworkers to cross back and forth between Canada and the United States and work at their trades.

Paul Diabo (third from left) and his attorneys outside the courthouse on July 8, 1926, just after the decision by Justice Bodine to dismiss the case against him.

SKYSCRAPERS

"What is the chief characteristic of the tall office building? At once we answer, it is lofty. . . . It must be tall. The force power of altitude must be in it, the glory and pride of exaltation must be in it."
—Louis Sullivan, architect

For thousands of years large structures had been built in the same way. The Great Pyramids of Egypt; the temples of Greece and Rome; the massive pyramids and palaces of ancient Mexico and Asia; the castles, cathedrals, and bridges of Europe; the United States Capitol and the Washington Monument were all built by piling stone upon stone. To raise a pyramid 476 feet high required the Egyptian builders to begin with a base 750 feet on a side. They then piled up over 2 million blocks of stone, some weighing as much as 15 tons.

Since the lower walls of a stone structure had to carry all the weight above, it was necessary to make them very thick. The world's tallest commercial building in 1889, the sixteen-story Monadnock Office Building in Chicago, required walls nearly 15 feet thick in the basement to support the masonry above. The thick walls only allowed for small windows, letting little light into the interior. The Chicago engineers were still working in a tradition going back to the towering cathedrals of medieval Europe. And they were reaching the height limit of masonry architecture. Inside the Monadnock Building, however, was something very new—a framework of cast iron posts and beams supporting the floors and carrying the load out to the walls.

A riveting gang high up on the Empire State Building, 1930.

As tall as the Monadnock was for its day, it was still not, technically, a skyscraper. That term first appeared in an article entitled "Chicago's Skyscrapers," in the January 13, 1889, issue of the *Chicago Tribune*. Typically, people use the term to describe any tall building, but engineers have a more precise definition, having more to do with the building's internal structure than its height. A skyscraper has a freestanding steel skeleton or frame enclosed by an outer skin. The walls carry no load; the frame does that. Since the walls carry none of the load, they can be made of lightweight material and, most important, can have many large windows. The first real skyscraper was the 138-foot tall, ten-story Home Insurance Building, built in Chicago in 1884 and designed by William Le Baron Jenney.

Jenney's bold new step in construction and design was actually based on ancient building methods. While traveling in the Philippines, he discovered that

Construction stages of a steel frame building, the Fair Store in Chicago, designed by architect William Le Baron Jenney, one of the originators of the skyscraper.

the natives built their houses on a bamboo frame—a "skeleton" frame—covered with woven thatch to keep out the weather. Since Jenney was trained in France, he may have also known about two buildings there constructed on a wrought iron framework. From these experiences, he came up with the idea of a strong metal cage built of wrought iron I-beams and cast iron columns bolted together. The frame would be hidden inside masonry walls that could be thinner because they carried none of the dead load of the floors.

Mr. Jenney's skyscraper is noted for another historical first. When the iron framework had reached the sixth floor, he received a letter from his iron supplier, the Carnegie-Phipps Steel Company of Pittsburgh. The letter announced that they were now rolling steel I-beams and asked Jenney's permission to substitute these for the wrought iron beams planned for the remaining four floors. Jenney agreed, making the Home Insurance Building the first made, at least partly, of structural steel. Jenney has since become known as "the father of the skyscraper."

New skyscrapers using Jenney's concepts soon followed so quickly it was hard to keep up with them. Chicago's Tacoma Building (1888-89) was the first to have a riveted skeleton. The Rand McNally Building (1889) became the first to have rolled steel beams and columns riveted together. The Masonic Temple (1890) with twenty-one stories of steel framing was, for a while, the tallest building in the world. Chicago was so closely identified with these innovations that "skyscraper" was defined in the dictionary as "a very tall building such as now are being built in Chicago."

Although the skyscraper was invented in Chicago, it eventually became a symbol of New York City. New York was a much older city and had in place more strict and inflexible building codes. If Jenney had wanted to build his daring design first in New York, the Building Department of New York City would surely have turned it down. Later, after the skyscraper had proved itself in Chicago, New York accepted the idea—just at the time the men of Kahnawake were booming out. The riveting of architectural steel brought many Mohawk ironworkers off of bridges and up into skyscrapers.

THE CHANGING SKYLINE

Try to imagine New York or, for that matter any city in the world, in, say, 1890. The tallest structures, towering above everything else, were church steeples. It had been that way for centuries. In New York, the tallest steeple, its apex 284 feet above the sidewalk on Broadway, was atop Trinity Church. People paid a penny to trudge up the stairs and look out in awe over the entire city, at thousands of buildings which, with the exception of church steeples, were not over six stories high. In those days before elevators, six stories was considered the maximum number of floors people would walk up. Then, across the street and just three years later, the Manhattan Life Insurance Company Building rose 344 feet into the air. Taller and taller buildings caused church steeples to disappear from the skyline. As one observer described it, "The spires that once had been the pinnacles of the city were soon like stalagmites on the floor of a cave." And it all happened in a single lifetime. Architectural historian Paul Goldberger explains why:

> The notion of height was to become the overriding image of New York City in the years after 1900, and thus, by extension, the image of all American cities growing to maturity. The idea that a city is primarily an agglomeration of small- to medium-sized buildings, made urban by their closeness, was pushed aside by the coming of the skyscraper. . . . A city showed its might by how many buildings it had and how many people were in it, and, more to the point, by how big these buildings could be made to be. Our very notion of what cities were was changed forever.

No sooner was the tallest building built than it was soon overtaken by a taller one, and then a taller one yet. The Woolworth Building (1913) reached 761 feet; 40 Wall Street (1930), 925 feet; the Chrysler Building (1930), 1,046 feet,

The Flatiron Building, one of New York City's most famous landmarks, under construction. When it was completed in 1902, the 22-story building was one of the tallest buildings in the city.

the Empire State Building (1931) reached 1,250 feet, and the World Trade Center (1972-73) 1,368 feet. Chicago took the lead again with the Sears Tower (1976) topping out at 1,450 feet. Then came the Petronus Twin Towers (1998) in Kuala Lampur, Malaysia, at 1,483 feet. Honors go to the Shanghai World Financial Center (2007) at 1,614 feet, and Taipei 101 (2004) at 1,671 feet, the Burj Khalifa, opened in 2010 in Dubai, reaches 2,717 feet into the sky. By the time you read this, a dozen even taller buildings will have been built or planned.

Is there a limit? Probably not. In the 1950s, architect Frank Lloyd Wright proposed a mile-high building for Chicago—that's 5,280 feet tall. Most engineers agreed it was possible, and Mohawk ironworkers would surely have vied for the honor of building it to the very top. But it was never built because, economically, it just didn't make sense.

BUILDING A SKYSCRAPER

Conway Jocks remembers, as a kid, following his father from job to job, beginning in 1930 with the biggest of all, the Empire State Building. "In those glory days of the old-timers there were three main divisions of labor in putting up a bridge or a skyscraper: they were the raising gangs, the fitting-up gangs, and the riveting gangs." Contemporary accounts of the work on the Empire State Building enable us to reconstruct the story of Conway and his father, beginning with their first day on the job. Actually, they arrived as the foundation work was finishing up, so they began skywalking by descending deep into a huge hole—the best place for a brand new punk to start on the job.

The first task for the raising gang is to erect the giant derricks that pick up heavy steel beams and girders, lift them up several stories, put them exactly where they belong, and hold them in position while they are temporarily fastened with bolts. The huge derricks arrive at the building site in pieces small enough to be carried through city streets on trucks. So the first work is to bolt all the sections together, like an oversized Erector Set. On large jobs, like the Empire State Building, several derricks will work together.

Meanwhile, the equipment arrives, most important the air compressors that power the rivet guns. (Hand riveting was replaced by pneumatic rivet guns at the turn of the twentieth century.) The job is now "ready for steel." The site begins to take on the feeling of a small city. Most days there will be 2,500 men at work here; sometimes there are as many as 4,000.

The arrival of the steel is timed with mathematical precision. There's no space on a city street to store all the materials needed at the job site. (In all, the Empire State Building required 303,000 tons of steel. It was cut to size at a "bridge shop" and put on flat cars and delivered to railroad yards in New Jersey. Then it was loaded onto barges and towed across the Hudson River to a wharf and waiting trucks.) The trucks are scheduled to arrive at the building site precisely at the time that a piece of steel is needed—30 trucks arriving and departing every hour, 250 each working day. Immediately, as the truck pulls to

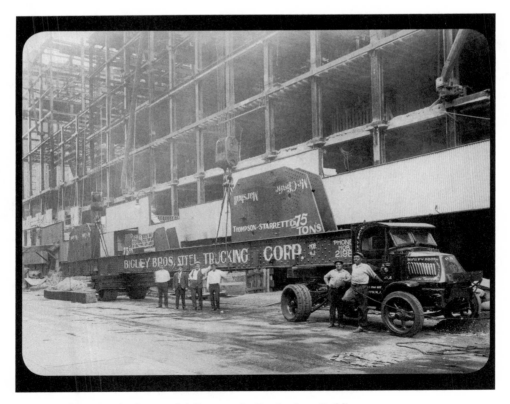

A truck makes a just-in-time steel delivery to the Empire State Building.

a stop, the derrick "hooks on" to the steel, lifting it directly from the truck bed to the connector waiting above.

The raising gang gets to work readying a two-story-high steel column to be lifted into place. Each piece of steel is numbered to correspond to the numbers on the architects' drawing. The raising gang must ensure that each piece goes into the right place. Heavy steel cable slings are dragged under the column and then slipped over the derrick hooks. A rigger raises his arm, index finger pointed upward, and with a circular motion signals the derrick operator to lift

Raise load   Lower load   Raise boom   Lower boom

Raise load small amount   Lower load small amount   Raise boom small amount   Lower boom small amount

Stop   Hold (dog) everything   Swing load or travel hand gives direction   Travel as directed

Raise load and lower boom   Lower load and raise boom   Hold load and raise boom   Track motions turning caterpillar

The noise on the job and the distances between workers made it impossible for workers and crane operators to communicate safely by voice, so hand signals became the language of ironworkers.

the column. Up comes 52 tons with no more effort than lifting a sheet of paper. As the rigger signals the direction the column is to go, the column glides slowly and then stops precisely where it is needed on the rigger's signal. Again, on signal, the column drops until, with a solid clunk, it sits down on the concrete foundation, right over the anchor bolts. This operation will be repeated over and over again the next few days, as 200 columns are bolted down to the foundation.

The steel climbs higher and higher, directed and controlled by the men doing the most dangerous work of all, the connectors. These are the guys who straddle and ride the girder being lifted off the truck and up into the air, swung around, and lowered into place, and then slip the temporary bolts into place as soon as the rivet holes line up—200, 500, 1,000 feet in the air. They shinny up columns and chin themselves up onto girders, their overall pockets loaded with 30 or 40 pounds of nuts and bolts. Tucked into their belt is a heavy spud wrench, its long handle tapered to a pointed end, a spud. The connector uses the spud end to align the holes as two pieces come together, so that he can easily slip in the temporary bolts. Then it is the riveter's turn to make the connections final. Rivet guns made the job a bit easier and faster, but no less dangerous. Conrad Jocks described the work of the Mohawk teams:

> The fitting-up gang tightens up the pieces with guy wires and turnbuckles, and they make sure they are plumb [perfectly vertical]. The bolters then put in some more temporary bolts. Now it's the turn of the four-man riveting gang consisting of a heater, a catcher, a bucker-up, and a riveter.
>
> The heater lays some wooden planks across a couple of beams, making a platform for the portable coal-burning forge in which he heats the rivets. The three other men hoist up a planked scaffold on which they're going to work. The scaffold is usually six 2 x 10 planks—three on each side of the steel—giving them just enough room to work. That is the most dangerous part. The three men now take positions on the scaffold, with the catcher and bucker-up on one side, the riveter on the other. On his platform the heater picks up a red-hot rivet off the coals

with tongs and tosses it to the catcher who snags it with a metal cone. I remember my dad saying, "If you can't catch the rivet, to hell with it." In other words it wasn't worth stretching for.

Meanwhile the bucker-up has unscrewed and removed one of the temporary bolts. The catcher takes the rivet out of his cone with his tongs and fits it into the hole, pushing in until the button head is flush with the steel on his side, then steps aside for the bucker-up who fits a dolly bar over the button head and holds it there, bracing the rivet. The riveter then presses the cupped head of his pneumatic hammer against the protruding stem-end of the rivet, which is still red-hot and malleable, and turns on the power. *Brrrrrrrrrrrp Brrrrrrrrrrrp.* It's almost that fast. This operation is repeated until every hole that can be reached from the scaffold is riveted up, after which the scaffold is then moved. The heater's platform stays in place until all the work within a rivet-tossing radius of thirty to forty feet is completed.

The men on the scaffold know each other's jobs and they're interchangeable. The riveter's job is bone shaking and nerve racking, and every so often one of the others swaps with him for a while.

Even today it is impressive how fast what was then the tallest building in the world went up. Imagine stopping on your way to school each morning to watch the work through a hole in the wooden fence put there especially for "sidewalk superintendents." If you had peeked in on the morning of April 7, 1930, you would have watched the first massive column going up.

Just a week later you would have seen the derricks swinging steel into place for the second floor! Your ears would have ached at the sounds of steel work—the *brrrrpbrrrp tat-tat-tat-tat brrrrrrrp brrrrrrp tat-tat* tattoo of dozens of pneumatic rivet guns, sledge hammers ringing against steel, the hum of the

Ironworkers on the Empire State Building direct the crane operator to raise a beam into place. By now these men are so high that cafeterias have been set up on upper floors because they wouldn't have time to descend for lunch.

electric elevator motors, the throbbing of the air compressors, the thrum and rumble of trucks arriving with their loads of steel, shouts, signal bells, shrieking whistles, chugging, puffing steam engines, the whir of the derricks, the clatter of cement mixers, the hissing of blacksmith's forges, the resounding thump of steel meeting steel, the hubbub of thousands of men at work.

In another week—just eighteen days after the first column went up—the derricks were lifting steel to the fourth floor. The steel was then being erected at the rate of 10,000 tons of steel per month. Down in the basement, plumbers, carpenters, masons, steam fitters, sheet metal workers, and electricians worked amidst piles of cement, sand, crushed rock, stacks of pipe, huge spools of wire, and tools.

May 5, 1930. Elevator constructers begin installing the guide rails for the sixty-six elevators.

June 5, 1930. Masons begin at the sixth floor putting up the granite and limestone skin. The spaces between the steel column and girders are walled with brick—10,000,000 bricks to be exact. The brick walls are the backing onto which the stone facing is cemented. The difference steel framing makes in the stonework is now clear. Because the facing is just a wall and does not support any of the weight of the building, it is only 4 to 8 inches thick. The masonry facing is now going up at the rate of a story a day. On one day, an entire floor was faced in just six hours. Materials new to architecture appear on the site—long strips of chrome-nickel steel trim and aluminum plates fill the spaces above and below each window, giving the exterior a glowing luster.

June 23, 1930. Steel is arriving at the twenty-sixth floor. The derricks have been moved up to the twenty-fifth floor. The poured concrete floors have begun catching up with the steel. When the floors are done, 1,700,000 cubic feet of concrete will have been mixed, hoisted up to each floor, and poured into forms. Temporary walls of rope netting are stretched around the building to protect the men from falling and being blown away by the high winds at this height.

July 21, 1930. One and a half months after the first steel column was raised

The Empire State Building reaches skyward and is already towering over the city, in this photograph taken from the Chrysler Building in 1931.

into position, forty stories tower above Broadway and 34th Street. Nearly three-quarters of the steel has been raised into position. The stonework is completed to the twenty-sixth floor. Work has begun on glazing the 6,400 windows. The ironworkers clamber about the steel, shirtless under the summer sun. Men of thirty different trades are at work. Ten miles of temporary pipes carry drinking water to thirsty workmen all the way to the top.

September 15, 1930. Topping out. The last piece of steel completes the eighty-sixth floor—placed by a Mohawk connector. It's taken only twenty-five weeks to complete all the steel work, except for the observation tower and mooring mast—twelve days ahead of schedule.

The masons have enclosed sixty-four floors in stone and aluminum. The goal is to have the building completely enclosed before winter sets in, all in a record-breaking time of 113 days. Work is progressing on connecting the 350,000 electric light sockets and receptacles with over 2 million feet of wire.

Winter/spring 1930–31. On rainy days, the top of the building disappears into the fog. An unimaginable variety of tasks go on inside the stone and aluminum sheathed walls. The building becomes a city in itself with a population of 25,000 workers. After the fast, dramatic work of raising the steel framework, the slow, careful details remain—building partitions, installing elevators and hoisting machinery, plastering walls, hanging doors, installing radiators, laying mosaic and marble floors, installing plumbing and electrical fixtures, painting, laying carpets, moving furniture into place—on and on.

May 1, 1931. The Empire State Building is finished and formally opened to the public. It will remain unchallenged as the world's tallest building for over forty years, until the completion of the World Trade Center's north tower in 1972.

Just another day's work on the Empire State Building.

MOHAWK MYTHS AND REALITIES

"A lot of people think Mohawks aren't afraid of heights; that's not true. We have as much fear as the next guy. The difference is that we deal with it better." –Kyle Beauvais, Mohawk ironworker

Mohawk ironworkers were "discovered" by most Americans sometime in the 1950s when articles about them began to appear regularly in popular magazines like *National Geographic, New Yorker,* and *Colliers,* and in the feature pages of newspapers. They were "Cowboys of the Skies," "Industrial Daredevils," and "Sky Boys," in articles that always had a *wow! gee whiz!* tone. Like Superman, they were credited with being able to leap tall buildings in a single bound and accomplish amazing, unbelievable feats of derring-do. After years of living quietly and unnoticed in their Brooklyn enclave, the Mohawks' new fame must have come as a surprise. As one young ironworker quipped, "I'm just glad we didn't go into plumbing. Nobody would be interested in us if we were plumbers."

Our awe of the ironworker surely comes in part from our own fear of heights. Most of us consider it just good common sense to stay off the scary places where ironworkers spend their working lives. The everyday experiences of a riveter or connector are the stuff of nightmares, enough to wake you trembling in a cold

Two men climb a tower at a construction site.

sweat. No normal person would go up THERE. Anyone who does what they do must be some kind of superhuman. W. A. Starrett, an engineer who became a famous skyscrapers builder, speaks for most of us when he says, "Looking up ten stories does not seem so high, but looking down—Ye gods! If there ever was an experience to bring the human body its sense of helplessness and despair, its agonies and terrors, it is the sensation felt by one who has not had training when he suddenly finds himself out on a narrow beam or plank, high above the ground and unprotected by a hand-hold of any kind; simply depending on his sense of balance and equilibrium."

When writer Jim Rasenberger was researching his book *High Steel*, he went to the top floors of a skyscraper under construction. He found most disconcerting "the absence of walls and ceiling. Without these bearings, the novice's brain balks, shooting an urgent message to brain receptors in his extremities. The gist of the message is DON'T MOVE!"

Acrophobia, the fear of heights, is a common fear. According to a 1999 Harris Poll, 23 percent of Americans—roughly 1 in 4—describe themselves as "very afraid" of heights. Acrophobia is, by the way, second only to ophidiophobia, fear of snakes. Psychologists have many explanations for the origins of acrophobia, but ironworkers tend not to pay much attention to them. As connector Mike Cherry puts it, "It doesn't matter much, because if you've got it you've got it, and if you mean to be an ironworker, you had better get over it."

Most of the stories about Indian ironworkers that emerged in the 50s were accurate and sensitively written, but along the way some myths crept into the writing. Repeated over the years, the myths soon took on the mantle of fact. There was the myth of the fearless Mohawk, innately sure-footed, born to walk the high steel. Under the subtitle "Indians Have Little Fear of Heights," a *National Geographic* writer considered the question: "Why did the Caughnawaga [Kahnawake] Mohawks take so eagerly to this spine-chilling high iron work? The answer seems to lie in a puzzling characteristic found in many North American Indian Tribes, and outstandingly in the Iroquois; they are almost completely lacking in fear of heights." An article in the *Industrial Bulletin*, published by the New York State Department of Labor, explained that "the Mohawks, alone among all Indian tribal groups, have an instinctive lack of fear of height." A

Herald-Tribune article referred to the "cool bravery and disdain for danger, two of the great characteristics of the Indian race." *Parade* magazine told its Sunday readers that the "Mohawks are famed for their catlike agility, tightrope walker's balance, and indifference to heights."

How much of the Mohawks' skill is innate and how much is learned? "This is a very basic question we don't have an answer to yet," admits Dr. Bernard Cohen, a neurologist and specialist in balance disorders. What neurologists do know is that people with acrophobia can be trained, by gradual exposure to higher and higher places, to overcome their fear. It may have to do with how we train our eyes to see what we want to see and don't want to see. Dr. Cohen is in some agreement with an explanation that appeared in *Bridgemen's Magazine* long before there were neurologists. "If it were possible for the average man to so concentrate his vision on the beam upon which he stands, that he could see nothing else than the beam," the writer speculates, "there would be no danger of falling. The moment he would catch a glimpse of the abyss on either side he would be gone." The writer is talking about the very complex relationship between the ears and the eyes, a relationship doctors don't fully understand yet. But, Dr. Cohen believes, "You can change how your eyes move depending on experience and circumstances."

Just watching Indians on high steel suggests something extraordinary about them. There's the famous photograph of eleven men sitting side-by-side high on a narrow beam above the city casually chatting and eating their lunch. Ironworkers tell stories of men so relaxed they fell asleep sitting on a narrow beam hundreds of feet in the air. Conway Jocks laughs as he recalls the antics of his gang on the Verrazano-Narrows Bridge: "The ironworkers made a game of dropping their lunch bags on steamers going under the span. The idea was to get the bag down the smoke stack." Jim Rasenberger tells about men he observed working on the Time Warner Center high above New York. One of them stopped in the middle of a girder to casually light a cigarette, another to count the cash in his wallet. Two men headed in opposite directions stopped out on a 10-inch-wide girder to share a joke and a laugh, and then just stepped around each other and continued on their way. "A young ironworker sprinted across a beam, taking the whole length of it in three or four strides, then leaped over a

Joe Jocks and fellow ironworkers taking their lunch break on the RCA Building (1932)—eight-hundred feet above the street.

two-foot wide gap onto the deck. He grabbed a tool and ran back exactly as he had come. He would either make a great ironworker, Rasenberger thought to himself, "or a dead one."

GOING IN THE HOLE

The facts tell a very different story about the Indians' lack of fear of heights. Falls, even for Mohawks, are inevitable. "You almost fall three or four times a day," says Mohawk ironworker Albert Stalk, Jr. "You don't even think about it until somebody reminds you later on. They'll say, 'I thought you were going in the hole today.'" Richard Hill recalls that both his father and his brother had taken falls several times. Most ironworkers have fallen at least once. And every time one falls, it shatters the myth of the sure-footed, invincible Indian ironworker.

Early ironworkers worked without any protection—no hard hats, no "tying on" with safety harnesses, no fall nets to keep a man from dropping "into the hole," no protection around the outside of the building to catch a man going over the side. A law passed early in skyscraper work required contractors to spread wooden planks on the floor below where the men were working so that, at most, a man would fall 12 or 15 feet. But contractors ignored the law, and there were apparently no inspectors in those days to check up on them.

You would think that the ironworkers themselves would have complained about the lack of protection, but danger was so much a part of what they did that it didn't occur to them. Many ironworkers actually resisted wearing safety harnesses, claiming it interfered with their freedom of movement, thus making the work more dangerous. It wasn't until the 1930s, with the building of the Golden Gate Bridge, that the American Bridge Company first issued every bridgeman a leather hard hat. For the first time, also, safety nets were strung underneath the bridge to catch falling workers. That simple precaution, unknown previously in the whole history of bridge building, saved nineteen lives.

It is no myth that ironwork was and is a dangerous job. Between 1900 and

1920, over 2,000 ironworkers were killed on the job. An issue of *Bridgemen's Magazine* reported in 1902 that New York City's Local 2 buried two men a week for six weeks. For much of the early twentieth century, two out of every one hundred ironworkers died on the job, and another two were permanently disabled each year. If you add up the numbers, you realize that in a local union of 1,000 members, 200 were killed and 200 more permanently disabled after ten years. After twenty years, 800 workers would have died or been permanently disabled. "It's a sad, gruesome, and only too truthful fact," a union official observed, "that no ironworker is considered to die a natural death unless he gets killed."

And the fearless Mohawks? Statistics show that as many Indian ironworkers die in proportion to their numbers as non-Indians. Most Mohawks can tell the same story about themselves or another Indian on the job that connector Leroy Ferguson tells. He was a connector, the most dangerous job of all, for twenty-five years: "I fell when I was climbing a column and an anchor bolt snapped. I rode the column down as you are told to do, and jumped off just before it hit the ground. But my foot landed on a stone and twisted until it broke. I was off for six months, but had to return t' prove to myself that I could do it.'" Leroy worked on one job in Michigan during the 1960s that killed seventeen ironworkers. Later, he had to quit after seriously injuring his back in another accident.

Stan Hill, from Six Nations, learned early the dangers of ironwork. He was working with his brother-in-law, Elmer Greene. "I had to save Elmer from falling on our first job together. He was cutting a section loose from a bridge that we were dismantling, when the iron knocked him off the top. I was close enough to reach out and grab the bib of his overalls and pull him back on top. Years later I saw my own son fall from the steel, not realizing it was him until I turned the fallen ironworker over."

Ironwork ranks third, after logging and fishing, for deaths on the job. "The erection of structural steel," according to the U.S. Bureau of Labor Statistics, "must be recognized as one of the most, if not the most, hazardous industrial operations." And still Mohawks do the work. Of the 340 members of Local 440 in Utica, New York, 270 are Mohawks. On the rolls of Local 40 in New York City are over 500 Indian ironworkers. The total number of Indian ironworkers in

the U.S. and Canada is somewhere around 7,500. A recent study revealed that in Kahnawake 70 percent of the working men were ironworkers. Of the retired workforce, 83 percent were ironworkers.

FEAR GIVES YOU THE EDGE

Do Indians find the work scary? You bet they do. "It's not that we don't fear heights," Mohawks will tell you. "It's that we respect heights." Conway Jocks is always wary. "A good ironworker is afraid of high places. I don't want to work with no fool who's not a little bit afraid of being up so high. It's the fear that gives you the edge, that keeps you alert. If you weren't afraid, at least a little, then you wouldn't have that edge. No, a Mohawk is afraid of heights just like the next guy. The difference is the Mohawk is willing to deal with it." Eugene Skye, says he starts each day on the job repeating several times to himself, "I ain't goin' to die today; why should I die today?"

Dealing with fear, then, is something Indians learn to do. Anthropologists have suggested that the trait was learned out of necessity. Indians were competing for relatively high paying jobs. If they couldn't go out on high steel, then they were unemployed or working at something paying much less. Ironworkers typically make about $35 an hour, adding up to $1,400 a week, or $65,000 to $70,000 a year. So, Mohawk men learned to cope with fear.

Walking the iron, then, was something every punk had to *learn*. "You may see an ironworker strolling along a girder up there," says Conway Jocks, "but it doesn't come automatically. It's not a sin if a beginner crawls along the girder with his feet locked on the flanges." Some punks walk the iron from the first day, but others begin by "cooning" the beam—straddling the beam with the feet firmly on the bottom flange, scooting along on the butt. Someday, he finds himself on a wide beam. Working up his courage, the punk stands up on the top flange, crouching low to the beam or "seagulling," walking with his arms

Connector Alec Mayo braces for the arrival of a steel beam. The Chrysler Building is in the distance.

straight out. He tries a few baby steps, and then a few more. Eventually, he's walking even narrow beams like an old timer—or maybe not. Some ironworkers get around their whole careers cooning. Seagulling, however, is considered bad form, though some old timers have done that their whole careers, as well.

So punks had to learn, but they didn't have to learn on their own. Older ironworkers took seriously their responsibility to train them. Joe Carl, a non-Indian ironworker, recalls how he learned to walk a beam from a Mohawk gang. "They walked across those steel beams as though they were nothing. And, as I was a young fella, they took me under their wing. 'Joe, look across there, look straight across to where you're walking; put one foot in front of the other—DON'T LOOK DOWN. And we will be behind you if you make a mistake.' One time I stepped on a greasy girder and slipped on it. They were on me so fast, I don't think I was hanging on that girder fifteen seconds."

Learning to walk a beam is only the beginning. Once he has the basic skill down, the ironworker has to get comfortable enough up there to actually get his work done. Then there's the rain, snow, searing heat, and freezing cold ironworkers have to deal with, and the constant wind. Wind is one of the first things a visitor to the upper stories notices. At street level, sheltered by all the surrounding buildings, it might be a calm day. Above, however, in the world without walls of the ironworkers, the wind will howl. Leroy Ferguson recalls that, as a connector, he had to walk on top, and the real enemy was the wind. You could never know for sure what it was doing. "I would be walking across a beam, leaning into the wind, and all of a sudden, the wind would quit and I'm left leaning into nothing."

Another problem is that the wind or your footfalls can cause a beam to vibrate and oscillate up and down and from side to side. Ironworkers call this "wow," and it's scary. Jake Swamp recalled experiencing wow the first time. "I learned that when you walk a long, narrow beam don't stop. The beam becomes rubbery, and if you stop it will throw you off balance." If you see an ironworker dashing across a beam, chances are he's trying to stay ahead of the wow.

Right: Two ironworkers. At right is Mohawk worker Anthony Goodleaf.

TRADITIONS OLD AND NEW

Anthropologists have several theories about why Mohawks are attracted to ironwork. None any longer suggest that it is hereditary or inborn. It is unlikely scientists working on the human genome will find a section of DNA to be labeled "high steel." Instead, some see the fast, dangerous, adventurous life of ironworking as the latest chapter in the Mohawk's long history as fierce warriors and courageous voyageurs. "I need to feel every muscle, every bone," says ironworker Art Cross, "the pain and the adrenalin. Only then do I feel powerful, and free!"

Ironworkers are seen by some as continuing a tradition begun centuries ago. Walking high steel, challenged every moment to make life or death choices, Mohawk men are following in the footsteps of their forebears who braved the perilous rapids of Canada's wild rivers as canoemen, rafters, and steamboat pilots. Richard Hill, who grew up in a Mohawk ironworking family agrees: "Ironwork is a traditional activity because it also fulfills a social and cultural need in our communities. Ironworkers of today, like the traders and trappers of the past, travel great distances seeking the adventure of the next job, and secure goods for their families back home."

Even in this new century, the role of tradition cannot be discounted. It's not that Indian workers up on high steel actually think of themselves moment to moment as warriors, canoemen, and rafters reborn. And it doesn't mean they need to wear feather headdresses and beaded moccasins on the job. But somewhere deep inside them is an awareness that in working the high steel they are somehow acting out their history.

They are keeping their old traditions alive by living new ones. Anthropologist Paul Ricoeur is someone who has thought and written a lot about tradition. "Our heritage," he observes, "is not a sealed package we pass from hand to hand, without ever opening, but rather a treasure from which we draw by the handful and which, by this very act, is replenished. Every tradition lives by grace of interpretation, and it is at this price that it continues, that is, remains living." What keeps traditions alive, then, is not doing the old things over and over again, long after they have lost their meaning. Traditions are kept alive by adapting them to modern life, expressing the old traditions in new ways.

So how does the Mohawk ironworker draw by the handful from his rich store of traditions? Telling stories is one way. The Indian oral tradition lives today not just in the telling and retelling of the ancient tales to each new generation, but in adding new ones. The latest heroes of Mohawk storytellers are legendary ironworkers, like the connector who bolted up more steel in one day than had ever been done before, or the hilarious antics of the new punk who froze like a statue out on the middle of a beam and had to be rescued.

The ironworker becomes, for his children, their teller of tales. The new stories, rather than being told around a campfire, are probably told to the family in the car on a weekend drive. The sites visited on these trips are the latest accomplishments of the Mohawk ironworkers, bridges, and buildings, and other structures that, perhaps, the father has worked on. Along the way, he regales his kids with stories about when he was a teenager, when at night he and his buddies would climb up into the trusses of old Black Bridge, a railroad bridge that crossed hundreds of feet above the St. Lawrence into Kahnawake. The object was to do the scariest things they could, like running screaming and hollering along the inches-wide top chord from one end to the other, watching their drink cans disappear into the blackness below. And there's the one about the kid who actually did wheelies on his bicycle along that top chord. A boy would fall every now and then. That was sad, but it didn't stop them from going back.

And then would come the lesson in the story. "We were scared," the father might say, "but being scared was the point. It's all right to be scared." Someday, the children, whose role now is to listen and remember, will tell these stories to their children, along with new stories of their own.

THAT'S WHERE THE WORLD OPENS UP

"There is a strong sense of tradition among most Indian ironworkers. There is a sense of family that connects this generation of ironworkers to the men who have lived and died on the steel." That's the way George Gilbert feels. George began work as a connector at seventeen and later taught himself to read and write the Mohawk language. Each day, after finishing work on the steel, he went back to his motel room to study Mohawk history and traditions that his generation wasn't taught. "We were always aggressors in battle. We always wanted a challenge. But pushing toward the sky, moving closer to the Creator, also brings out a spiritual side. It's like you're at the top of the world. You're like an eagle."

For many ironworkers, it's the challenge of the job that's attractive. As Jake Swamp puts it: "To accomplish something that has a lot of fear tied to it, and be able to get beyond it, that's where the world opens up." The Mohawks often talk about growing by taking risks. Like many Indian ironworkers, Ron LaFrance is articulate in expressing what he gets from the work. "As a connector, I found the work was thrilling, dangerous, but very rewarding personally. There are many moments when you have to overcome your fears, and in doing so you rise to an emotional plateau. Then you go on to the next challenge, looking for the next high."

Although there are other kinds of work available to Mohawk men, including jobs that actually pay more—many ironworkers have college degrees—these are not considered "real work." For a job to qualify as "real work," it must be hard, physical labor. "You have to accept that you will work hard," Ron LaFrance explains. "You have to like to work hard. Working hard became a game. By giving the most of yourself, you could tease others about their effort. Gangs had a friendly but serious competition to see who could get the most done each day. It was a gamble each day, through snow, rain, and heat, but the sense of accomplishment made it all worthwhile."

"Real work" is also work few people would want to do. Mohawk ironworkers are proud of the ways their job distinguishes them from all others. They are different from most of us. When you walk across a six-inch-wide piece of steel eighty stories above Midtown Manhattan and the people and cars way below you look like tiny specks, you know you are different.

For some, like Stan Hill, the motivation might be the political realities of America: "The white man looked down on Indians for so long, we got to believe it ourselves. Iron work was a way out, a way to become someone, to compete, to beat the white man . . . to compete with the society that we are stuck with." His son Rick Hill also sees ironworking as proof of his worth. "Mohawk ironworkers do know what they like about the job. It is the thrill of doing something that most people couldn't and doing it better than those that try. Each steel skyscraper and expansive bridge is testimony of the Indian spirit to survive, to seek, and to achieve."

RITES OF PASSAGE

Most traditions include ritual objects, and so does ironworking. The ritual objects of the Mohawk ironworker are his tools—leather belt, hardhat, rope set, bolt pin, hammer, bolt bag, and spud wrench. Over the years, they are passed on from grandfather, to father, to son, to grandson, respected and treated as

Ironworkers' tools

the most precious of a family's heirlooms—particularly if they come from the mother's side of the family.

"The Belt," is an especially powerful object, worn tilted at a precise angle on the hips. When not in use, it is hung in a special place, not to be touched by children or women. Boys know not to handle their fathers' tools until given permission, and that permission comes only when they are of age, physically and emotionally. Men recall the first time they put on their belt as a transforming experience, the moment when they ceased to be boys and became men. Anthropologists refer to rituals like climbing on bridges at night and earning the right to put on an ironworker's belt as rites of passage.

Despite all that comes of being an ironworker, chances are a young Mohawk today will be discouraged from becoming one. Visitors to Kahnawake have observed a strange conflict among fathers. They are proud to be ironworkers or retired ironworkers, a skill that gives them considerable status in the community. They ridicule men who are not ironworkers. And yet, they discourage their boys from entering the trade, urging them instead to continue their education or find work that is less stressful, pointing out that most ironworkers are worn out, scarred, ache-ridden old men by their forties. A boy can't help but notice the cumulative effects of years of hard high steel work, the lined, weathered faces, the hunched backs, missing fingers, and limping gaits. In a survey of eighty men at Kahnawake, all but two said they did not want their sons to do ironwork.

But Mohawk sons are no different from most young men, in that they disregard the wishes of their fathers. This, too, is a rite of passage. Because he graduates from high school at seventeen and cannot join the union until he is eighteen, a young man uses that year to earn the money he will need to get started in his new career, to pay for union membership, a belt and tools, travel expenses, perhaps a car, and to live on until he gets a job and his first paycheck. The young man knows not to ask his family to pay these expenses. His ability to take these first important steps toward his chosen career entirely on his own means he has passed the first test, and he is ready to be an ironworker. He has successfully accomplished yet another rite of passage. And he has signaled his independence. As one Kahnawake mother described her reaction to her son's choice: "I opposed him to the very end. He stayed home for a few months and then decided to go, despite what I thought about it. When he made that decision, I knew then that he was ready to go, and I supported him. That's when a boy is ready to go out on his own, when he's ready to stand up to his mother."

BREAKING AWAY

Anthropologist David Blanchard was privileged to observe how the drama of a young man's coming of age played out in one Kahnawake family. Here is the story he tells about what happens after a young man announces to his family his decision to leave them and head for New York to become an ironworker.

> The father expressed complete opposition, yet the young man persisted. The mother and sisters tried to help to prepare for the departure while the father sat sullenly in his favorite chair, refusing to offer his son any words of advice, assistance, or encouragement. The young man had a new belt that he had purchased, some new tools, and an old bolt pin that had belonged to his maternal grandfather.
>
> While the women of the family continued to make sandwiches to be taken on the trip to New York, and to pack clothes, the young man retired to the family room where he cleaned his tools and re-adjusted his new belt, for the fifth or sixth time. His younger brother was present for this ritual, along with four of the neighborhood kids. The five of them sat around the young man, with wide open eyes, asking questions about the job, destination, and how much money would he be making. The young man offered answers to these questions as if he were an old pro. In fact, he had never been on a steel job and he had no assurances of work in New York.
>
> When this young man's friend's car pulled up in front of his house, the horn honked, and the passengers shouted for him to get moving. The boy's moment had arrived. His mother forced

a kiss on her son and the sisters held back their tears. The father remained seated. Finally, this boy-turned-man picked up his gear and left the house. The car honked its horn once more and pulled away. Unbeknownst to the family, the father had risen from his chair, and stepped to the front window. As his son and his friends pulled away, he raised his hand in a wave, and a faint smile passed over his lips.

David concludes with the story's happy ending. "This young man got a job working with his friends who showed him the ropes and broke him into the job. He spent his first few weeks 'tying rods,' but within a month was connecting steel. In the course of the year, the young man worked in Ohio, New York, New Hampshire, and California. Now, when he returns home, his father wants to know why he is not out working."

Above: A contemporary Mohawk ironworker on site in Harlem, New York City.

Right: Some Mohawk ironworkers place a feather in their hard hat as a symbol of their Native American identity.

AUTHOR'S NOTE

This book began with a journey, starting at home in Northern California, in the pine, oak, maple, and Douglas fir forests shading the foothills of the Yolla Bolly Mountains. "Yolla Bolly" is an Indian word meaning "snow-covered high peak." The land up there has been for eons the home of the Wailaki people. Another tribe, the Yukis, lived down in Round Valley, a separation maintained to this day. They lived in wickiups made of bent saplings thatched with grasses and built round ceremonial houses some 40 feet across. Their descendants, my neighbors, hunt deer and bear, fish for salmon in the creeks and streams running to Eel River, and walk the same forest paths and meadows as their ancestors did.

From this magical place, I headed for Montreal. My ultimate destination was the community of Kahnawake, what Canadians call a "reserve," on the south bank of the St. Lawrence River. I had no expectations for what I would find, so going there that first morning had the real feel of adventure. My writing takes me to places like this, places I would probably never get to otherwise but now count among my favorite travel experiences. There's nothing grand about Kahnawake, but it is one of those places I'll never forget.

Soon my trip from the heart of Montreal to Kahnawake had taken on the routine of a commute. Dodging traffic to cross the busy streets, passing through the doors of the Mont Royal Metro station, I would immediately be caught up in the surging crowd, immersed in fragments of French conversation, hustled shoulder to shoulder down the escalator, and carried out onto the platform. Trains, one after the other, rumbled to a stop and then, accelerating, disappeared into the dark of the subway tube. I settled down in the hard plastic seats of a silvery car speeding me toward Angrignon, the end of the line. There, a Mikie's Cab came to get me, behind the wheel each day a different Mohawk driver.

Shé:kon (it's pronounced "say-go"), I would greet the driver with one of the Mohawk phrases I had learned. Shé:kon, he would answer, amused at hearing his language spoken with a white guy's accent but pleased that I was trying. The "driver," I learned, was never just a driver. One was a sculptor who exhibited in galleries throughout America and Canada. He told me about driving around to quarries throughout New England to get the hunks of stone he wanted. Another told me of his work on "the Big Dig." Freeways, which had once passed over and through downtown Boston, were now in tunnels passing quietly, unseen under the city. It was the largest urban building project ever. "I didn't walk high up on red steel," he told me, "but I sure carried a lot of it." His job was to move and position long, heavy lengths of reinforcing rods, rebar, that would eventually be buried in concrete. And he referred to the Indians who do this work as "basket weavers."

I soon realized that not all the stories I had come to Kahnawake for were on the shelves and in the file drawers at the Kanien'kéhaka Raotitiohkwa Cultural Center Library. The personal stories began the moment I stepped into a cab. When I confessed to one driver that I tremble in fear atop a six-foot stepladder, he told me how he got used to working high up. "Luckily for me, the first morning I went to work with my father and uncle we started on the ground, down in a deep hole. So I got used to the heights one story at a time until I was way up there, five hundred feet up." The words "five hundred feet up" sent a shudder through my body.

On one of my morning trips, when I mentioned Mohawk steelworkers, the driver corrected me. "Steelworkers are the guys who make the steel," he explained. "Ironworkers are the guys who put it up." Another morning, it was I who got to tell a story. The driver was a young man, just graduated from high school. When he asked me why I was coming to Kahnawake, I explained I was researching a book on the Mohawk ironworkers. When I mentioned, in passing, the Quebec Bridge disaster, it became clear he hadn't heard the story and asked me to tell him what happened. I didn't have time to finish it before we drove up to the entrance to the Cultural Center. That evening, when I called Mikie's for a ride back to Montreal, the same young man showed up. He had made sure he got my call so that I could finish the story.

These stories bridged the abrupt transition between the frenetic, high-tech subway in Montreal and the little town that came into view each day as we crossed the Mercier Bridge arching over the St. Lawrence River. Kahnawake looks no different from any of the hundreds of little villages you'd see driving through eastern Canada and the United States. With its white church steeple rising above a cluster of neat houses, it looks not much changed from photographs I've found of the village a century ago. Only when you get closer and see the TV dishes on the houses, the cars and pickup trucks, do you realize that you are not in another time. When you come to a stop at a cross street marked by a red octagonal sign that says *Testa'n*, you know you are in another place.

Arriving at the Cultural Center, I wished that the drive and the stories could go on and on. "*O:nen ki'wáhi*," I would say to the ironworker/cab driver, "goodbye for now." "*Sataten'nik—n:raren*," he would reply, "take care of yourself."

At first, these comings and goings seemed a pleasant and informative way to get to where I was going and back. But then I realized that it was more than that, a lot more. In my own small way, I was experiencing firsthand what the life for the Mohawks has been for over a century now, moving back and forth between their quiet village and the great, noisy, boisterous cities of the world, all the time never losing sight of who they are. Although the jobs the men described were different, the stories they told had a singular quality—every word was spoken with pride. In their voices I heard, "I have been on the tallest buildings and the longest bridges. I was there, working hard, and we had the best gang on the job, a Mohawk gang, and we did good work. And, yeah, it's dangerous, but, you know . . ."

The Cultural Center, I discovered, is more than an expertly organized museum and archive for the study of an old and great nation, the Kanien'kéhaka, the "People of the Flint." Walking down the halls, I would stop at the open door of a classroom and listen to a language lesson. The adults in the class were learning to speak Mohawk, much as children do in school, beginning with simple everyday conversations. Some were parents eager to keep up with their children who are in the reserve's elementary "immersion" schools, where only Mohawk is spoken. But, I realized, something more was going on as well. They were reclaiming an ancient heritage, in the Mohawk way, finding a meeting of the old and the new.

Watching Tommy Deer, *Teyowisonte*, beautifully illustrating the ancient tales of his people on a computer and Martin Loft, *Akwiranoron*, an accomplished, talented photographer deftly copying the images of ironworkers onto a CD for me to take home, I suddenly understood. The Mohawk are people of the now; they have always been people of the now. I understood how Tommy's and Martin's ancestors could so readily put down their oars, travel to distant unfamiliar cities, climb out onto a high steel girder, pick up a rivet gun, and build the world's tallest buildings and longest bridges.

GLOSSARY

abutment a support at each end of a bridge built of stone or, later, concrete, which carries the load of the bridge to the ground

alloy a combination of two or more metals that creates a new metal with improved qualities, such as stainless steel

anchor arm the arm of a cantilever bridge that extends from the abutment to the main post on the river bank which, during construction, supports the cantilever arm extending out into the river

beam a horizontal structural member

Bessemer steel steel created by a process in which oxygen is blown through molten iron to burn out impurities

cantilever a structure that is free at one end and anchored or counterbalanced at the other end

cantilever arm the arm of a cantilever bridge that extends out from the main post

channel span the clear span between two piers standing in midstream

chord the horizontal structural members running the full length of a truss along the top and bottom

compression the force acting on a structural member that tends to squeeze it and make it shorter

compressive strength the ability of a material to withstand being squeezed or crushed

dead load the load on a structure caused by its own weight

deck the floor of a bridge

eyebar long, narrow bridge tension members connected through eyes or round holes at each end

falsework temporary supports that hold up a bridge until it is finished and can stand on its own

fatigue wear caused by bending, twisting, and vibrating structural materials until they fail

flange the flat top and bottom surfaces running the length of an I-beam

girder a wood, iron, or steel beam that works as a main support for a bridge or building

I-beam a steel girder with a cross section that looks like a capital letter *I*

latticing a zigzag pattern of iron or steel bars and angles that tie the individual pieces of a girder together

live load the load on a bridge caused by the traffic across it—cars, pedestrians, and, especially, the acceleration and braking forces of locomotives and trains—and wind

metallurgy the science and study of metals, ore refinement, and alloys

pier intermediate supports for long-span bridges

pin connected a type of bridge construction in which the main beams and posts are connected with large pins, usually threaded and fastened with nuts

rebar long steel rods embedded in concrete for reinforcement

shear a force, such as wind, acting across a structure perpendicular to the face of the structure

steel refined iron alloyed with carbon and sometimes nickel, vanadium, and other metals, which has greater strength and resistance to wear than either cast or wrought iron

strain the amount a member is stretched and deformed under load

stress the intensity of the load on a member, usually expressed as pounds per square inch

suspension bridge a bridge carried by cables or chains running continuously between anchorages at each end

tensile strength the ability to withstand being stretched and torn apart

tension the force pulling on a member tending to stretch and elongate it

traveler a movable structure with hoists that moves structural pieces out to the end of the bridge under construction and lifts them into place

truss a structure made up of posts and beams arranged in the shape of triangles and designed to carry tension and compression forces without bending

wrought iron iron with a low carbon content worked under a hammer to produce an metal that is less brittle and more malleable than cast iron, best for structural members under tension

SOURCES

Baughman, Michael. *Mohawk Blood.* New York: Lyons & Burford, 1995.

Berger, Meyer. "Dodgers, By Leaving, Probably Saved Colony of Mohawks Skilled on High Steel Jobs." *New York Times*, November 4, 1957.

Betancourt, Paul. *Haudenosaunee: People of the Longhouse.* Washington: National Museum of the American Indian, Smithsonian Institution, 2001.

Birkmire, William H. *The Planning and Construction of High Office Buildings.* New York: John Wiley & Sons, 1898.

Black, Archibald. *The Story of Bridges.* New York: Whittlesey House, 1936.

Blanchard, David S. *High Steel: The Kahnawake Mohawk and the High Construction Trade.* Unpublished ms., Department of Anthropology, University of Chicago, 1981.

———. "Introduction," in L. O. Armstrong, *Hiawatha the Mohawk. Kahnawake*, Quebec: Kanien'kéhaka Raotitiohkwa Press, 1981.

———. *Seven Generations : A History of the Kanien'kéhaka.* Kahnawake, Quebec: Kahnawake Survival School, 1980.

Bonvillain, Nancy. *The Mohawk.* New York: Chelsea House, 1992.

Cherry, Mike. *On High Steel: The Education of an Ironworker.* New York: Quadrangle, 1974.

———. *Steel Beams & Iron Men.* New York: Four Winds Press, 1980.

Condit, Carl W. *American Building: Materials and Techniques from the First Colonial Settlements to the Present.* Chicago: University of Chicago Press, 1968.

———. *The Chicago School of Architecture.* Chicago: University of Chicago Press, 1964.

Conly, Robert L. "Mohawks Scrape the Sky." *National Geographic*, July 1952.

Cory, David Monroe. *Within Two Worlds.* New York: Friendship Press, 1955.

Crane, Alison. "Reflections on Native American Identities." *Edwardsville Journal of Sociology* 1 (2001).

DeJonge, A. E. Richard. *Riveted Joints.* New York: The American Society of Mechanical Engineers, 1945.

"Details of Families: Married Men Killed." No. 319388. (facsimile of typewritten notes, n.d.) Kanien'kéhaka Raotitiohkwa Cultural Center Library.

Douglas, George H. *Skyscrapers: A Social History of the Very Tall Building in America.* Jefferson, NC: McFarland & Company, 1996.

Duffy, Peter. "The Mohawks of Brooklyn." *Brooklyn Bridge*, March 1999.

Dupré, Judith. *Bridges.* New York: Black Dog & Leventhal, 1997.

———. *Skyscrapers*. New York: Black Dog & Leventhal, 1996.

Freilich, Morris. "Cultural Persistence Among the Modern Iroquois." *Anthropos 53.*

Garcia, Maria. "Dance Honors Courage of the Steelworkers," in *Guide to Indian Country: Windspeaker's Aboriginal Tourism Suplement.* n.d.

Gies, Joseph. *Bridges and Men.* New York: Doubleday, 1963.

Glasser, Jeff. "High and Mighty: Race for the Sky,." *US News and World Report/Special Edition.* n.d.

Goldberger, Paul. *The Skyscraper.* New York: Alfred Knopf, 1981.

Goldenweiser, Alexander A. "Hanging Flower of the Iroquois." In *American Indian Life*, edited by Elsie Clews Parsons. Lincoln: The University of Nebraska Press, 1922.

Haley, D. B. "Local Union No. 87" (letter), *The Bridgemen's Magazine.* January 1908.

L'Hébreux, Michel. *Le Pont de Quebec.* Sillery: Septentrion, 1986.

Heuer, Jorg. "Himmelfahrtskommando." *Playboy*, April 1999 (German edition).

Hill, Richard. *Skywalkers: A History of Indian Ironworkers.* Ontario: Woodland Indian Cultural Center, 1987.

Jocks, Conway. *Kahnawake Ironworkers.* Kahnawake: Kanien'kéhaka Onkwawén:na Raotitiohkwa (interview), June 15, 2001.

Kanien'kéhaka Raotitiohkwa Cultural Center. *Of Men and Steel: Kahnawake and the Construction Industry.* n.d.

Middleton, William D. *The Bridge at Quebec.* Bloomington: Indiana University Press, 2001.

Mitchell, Joseph. "The Mohawks in High Steel," in *Up in the Old Hotel.* New York: Vintage, 1992.

Morgan, Alfred. *The Story of Skyscrapers.* New York: Farrar & Rinehart, 1934.

Moudry, Roberta, ed. *The American Skyscraper: Cultural Histories.* Cambridge: Cambridge University Press, 2005.

Rasenberger, Jim. *High Steel: The Daring Men Who Built the World's Greatest Skyline.* New York: HarperCollins, 2004.

Reid, Gerald F. *Kahnawake: Factionalism, Traditionalism, and Nationalism in a Mohawk Community.* Lincoln: University of Nebraska Press, 2004.

Richter, Daniel K. *Facing East From Indian Country: A Native History of Early America.* Cambridge: Harvard University Press, 2001.

Ricoeur, Paul. "Structure and Hermeneutics," in *The Conflict of Interpretations*, edited by Don Ihde. Evanston: Northwestern University Press, 1974.

Rose, William T. "Mohawk Indians Are World Famous for Their Skills in High Steel." *Industrial Bulletin.* New York State Department of Labor, October 1961.

Royal Commission. *Quebec Bridge Inquiry Report.* 2 vols. Ottawa, 1908.

Rustige, Rona. *Tyendinaga Tales.* Kingston: McGill-Queens University Press, 1988.

Schneider, C. C. *Quebec Bridge Inquiry.* Ottawa: Royal Commission Report, Vol. 1, 1908.

Shepherd, Roger. *Skyscraper The Search for an American Style 1891-1941.* New York: McGraw-Hill, 2003.

Simmons, David A. "The Continuous Clatter: Practical Field Riveting." *The Journal of the Society for Industrial Archeology.* 22:2 (1997).

Snow, Dean R., Charles T. Gehring, and William A. Starna. *In Mohawk Country: Early Narratives About a Native People.* Syracuse: Syracuse University Press, 1996.

———. *The Iroquois.* Oxford: Blackwell Publishers, 1998.

Starrett, W. A. *Skyscrapers and the Men Who Build Them.* New York: Charles Scribner's Sons, 1928.

Steinman, David B., and Sara Ruth Watson. *Bridges and Their Builders.* New York: Dover Publications, 1957.

Talese, Gay. *The Bridge.* New York: Harper & Row, 1964.

Taliman, Valerie. "Mohawk Ironworkers at Ground Zero: A Tradition of Courage." *American Indian.* Washington: National Museum of the American Indian, Smithsonian Institution, 2002.

Thomas/West/Westlaw. Circuit Court of Appeals, Third Circuit. McCandless, *Commissioner of Immigration v. United States ex rel. Diabo.* Nr. 3672, March 9, 1928.

———, District Court, E.D. Pennsylvania. *United States ex rel. Diabo v. McCandless.* Nr. M-54, March 18, 1927.

Tree of Peace Society. *The Great Law of Peace and the Constitution of the United States.* n.d.

Waddell, J. A. L. *De Pontibus: A Pocket-Book for Bridge Engineers.* New York: John Wiley & Sons, 1905.

Waite, Diana S., editor. *Architectural Elements: The Technological Revolution.* Princeton: The Pyne Press, n.d.

Weitzman, David. *Traces of the Past: A Field Guide to Industrial Archaeology.* New York: Charles Scribner's Sons, 1980.

———. *Windmills, Bridges & Old Machines: Discovering Our Industrial Past.* New York: Charles Scribner's Sons, 1982.

York, Geoffrey, and Loreen Pindera. *People of the Pines.* Boston: Little, Brown, 1991.

EXCERPT NOTES

p. 5 Dean R. Snow et al., *In Mohawk Country: Early Narratives About a Native People.*

pp. 7–8 *Ibid.*

p. 9 Alexander A. Goldenweiser, "Hanging Flower of the Iroquois," in *American Indian Life.*

pp. 10–12 Snow, *op. cit.*

p. 15 Kanien'kehaka Raotitiohkwa Cultural Center, video interview.

pp. 16–17 David Blanchard, *High Steel! The Kahnawake Mohawk and the High Construction Trade.*

pp. 17–18 *Ibid.*

p. 18–19 David Blanchard, *Seven Generations: A History of the Kanien'kéhaka,*

p. 20 *Ibid.*

p. 22 Kanien'kéhaka Raititiohkwa Cultural Center, interview transcript.

p. 34 Peter Duffy, *The Mohawks of Brooklyn.*

p. 56 Maria Garcia, *Guide to Indian Country.*

pp. 58–59 Kanien'kéhaka Raotitiohkwa Cultural Center, interview transcript.

pp. 62–63 Gay Talese, *The Bridge.*

p. 64 *Ibid.*

p. 65 Robert L. Conly, "The Mohawks Scrape the Sky," *National Geographic* (July, 1952).

p. 69–70 David Blanchard, *Seven Generations : A History of the Kanien'kéhaka.*

p. 73 Thomas/West/Westlaw, 18 F.2d 282, *United States ex rel Diabo v. McCandless*, No. M-54 (March 18, 1927).

p. 74 Paul Goldberger, *The Skyscraper.*

p. 78. *Ibid.*

pp. 83–84 Kanien'kéhaka Raotitiohkwa Cultural Center, interview transcript.

p. 91 William T. Rose, "Mohawk Indians Are World Famous for Their Skills in 'High Steel.'"

pp. 107–108 David Blanchard, *High Steel! The Kahnawake Mohawk and the High Construction Trade.*

PHOTO CREDITS

FRONT COVER: Stephen Simpson, Getty Images; **BACK COVER**: Lewis Hine, George Eastman House; **TITLE PAGE:** Lewis Hine, George Eastman House; **DEDICATION/TABLE OF CONTENTS**: David Grant Noble; **FRONTISPIECE**: James Karales, Library of Congress; **2**: David Grant Noble **3**: Kanien'kéhaka Onkwawén:na Raotitiohkwa (KOR); **7**: Bibliotéque Nationale Paris; **8**: Bibliotéque Nationale Paris; **10**: David Weitzman; **13**: Bibliotéque Nationale Paris; **21**: Collection of the Library and Archives of Canada; **24**: KOR; **26–27**: KOR; **30**: Wilfred Lineham, *Textbook of Mechanical Engineering*, 1902; **31**: *Engineering*, December, 1900; **33**: Todd France; **35**: Hagley Musem and Library; **38**: National Archives of Canada **39**: (top) Hagley Museum and Library; (bottom) National Archives of Canada; **40–41**: National Archives of Canada; **46–47**: National Archives of Canada; **48**: National Archives of Quebec; **51**: KOR; **52**: KOR; **55**: William Middleton; **57**: KOR; **60–61**: KOR; **66**: KOR; **73**: KOR; **75**: Lewis Hine, George Eastman House; **76**: *Industrial Chicago*, Godspeed Publishing, 1891; **79**: New York Public Library; **81**: KOR; **82**: Richard Hill; **85**: Museum of the City of New York; **87**: Lewis Hine, George Eastman House; **88**: Lewis Hine, George Eastman House; **90**: David Noble; **94–95**: Bethlehem Steel; **98**: KOR; **101**: David Grant Noble; **105**: Todd France; **108**: Todd France; **109**: David Grant Noble.

ACKNOWLEDGMENTS

There is only one name on the cover, but I have relied on several people to help tell my story. I got off to a good start with a visit to the resource center at the National Museum of the American Indian, where Ellen Jamieson recommended people to talk to and good books to read. Then, at Kahnawake, Tommy Teyowisonte Deer welcomed me to the Kanien'kéhaka Onkwawén:na Raotitiohkwa Cultural Center library and introduced me to his community. Martin Akwiranoron Loft helped me select images from the Center's archives and sent me home with a CD full of historical photographs, which enliven these pages. More images came from Peter Brill of the National Museum of the American Indian, and new perspectives from a visit with librarian Virve Wiland of the Woodland Cultural Center. Samuel Ayelsworth took on the roll of my legal researcher and expertly tracked down documents related to *McCandless vs. Diabo* and the Jay Treaty. I got an insider's view of what it's like to work on high steel from Richard Hill's splendid *Skywalkers: A History of Indian Ironworkers*, and from David Blanchard's *High Steel: The Kahnawake Mohawk and the High Construction Trade—* wonderful, poignant, vivid glimpses into workers' family life. Todd France and David Grant Noble graciously offered up their photographs, powerful images evocative of the hard, dangerous work. And then there is William Middleton. Bill gladly became my consultant on matters of structural engineering and bridge design, was always ready with answers to my questions, and made available the huge collection of photographs he had painstakingly assembled for his definitive study, *The Bridge at Quebec.*

INDEX